The
GATHERING
BUNKER

Golfing Short Stories

Kevin Pakenham

LITTLE, BROWN AND COMPANY

A *Little, Brown* Book

First published in Great Britain in 1996
by Little, Brown and Company

Copyright © 1996 by Kevin Pakenham

A CIP catalogue record for this book
is available from the British Library.

ISBN: 0 316 87730 1

Typeset in Plantin by M Rules
Printed and bound in Great Britain by
Clays Ltd, St Ives plc

Little, Brown and Company (UK)
Brettenham House
Lancaster Place
London WC2E 7EN

The
GATHERING
BUNKER

Contents

The
GATHERING
BUNKER

Teeing Off

'You're up, Jim,' said the sales director of our unit. It sounds easy enough to an accomplished golfer of many years' experience, but to me, making my way in the world, it had all the joy of wedding bells to a teenage father.

I made my way forward, trying to swing my club non-chalantly, and leant down to tee my ball up on its peg. To my surprise, after a wobble or two it remained there and I took my stance.

A corporate day like this one is a chance for a duffer, like I was then, to play on one of the great courses. It probably makes your mouth water just to think of it, but in my case my mouth was like the bunker on the seventh. If I told you I was playing off twenty-four you'd think I was a bandit, but in practice I was all rabbit.

Anyway, the thing about a great course is that they're awfully particular about their tees, especially the first tee. So I stood there, my muscles which had felt like jelly now turning to stone, and I looked in misery at the little notice which proclaimed NO PRACTICE SWINGS.

'Come on, Jim, show us the way.' Time passed. The sales director assessed me with good humour. His eyes indulgent, he stood hands on hips trying to strike a masterful pose, made somewhat difficult by his modest height. He was a hero in my eyes. He had backed me, given me the job of junior sales manager, had brought me on, and had paid me the ultimate compliment a few weeks earlier: 'Why don't you come on the corporate golf day? You play, don't you?'

Even then my throat went dry as I said, 'Certainly, Mr Burton, I'd be pleased to.' Then, after a pause, 'Though I'm not that good.'

'What do you call "not that good"? Can you break ninety?'

'Just about,' I choked.

'Well, you'll have no trouble, old son, and Stafford Spa is a course you'll never forget.' He was at least right about that.

I choked then and I was choking now, standing far too upright, my legs too straight, my feet rooted to the spot, and worst of all my hands raw from the hundreds of practice drives I had had the week before.

Exams, girlfriends, first days at school, first evenings out, all were as nothing compared to this moment. And why was I there? Was it really love of the game? Perhaps I had the faintest whiff of that opium which would come to dominate my later years, that awful replacement for human experience, that anti-social narcotic masquerading as a game. But I have to tell you that if I hadn't been a young man in search of gainful employment, I wouldn't have been within a thousand miles of that place, with all its cool conventions, its bonhomie and its underlying pulse of religious experience. As the great Wodehouse said, in later years women discover God and men discover golf.

But it was not later years for me. A healthy young man with normal appetites and enthusiasms, of one thing I was sure: no man had ever won a girlfriend on a golf course. I was, as you may know, wrong. You can meet almost anybody and anything on a golf course. But I was there simply as a career proposition, and a pretty good one at that, or so I thought until I actually stood on that tee, club in hand, a stone statue in the light drizzle, surrounded by the dark, sad pines of Surrey.

You've all seen those terrible shows on television which give clips in slow motion of some serious event going completely wrong. The newscaster getting the giggles, the birthday cake being dropped into the birthday boy's lap, the baby throwing up over Daddy's head, and the rookie golfer taking back his driver in laboured manner and missing.

Well, I didn't. I wish I had. I was prepared for that. 'Just practising,' I would have said. And someone would have said, 'Don't let the Secretary see,' and I would have said, 'Oh, I forgot.'

But I didn't miss. I had said to myself, so long as you get it away, no one will notice. But I was wrong. I had teed it up and I swiped, just like I had been practising, but I had teed it up too high and I had swiped too fast. My club went out like a fishing rod, and then across and under, and the ball soared heavenward.

Gladys is not a particularly common appellation these days, and maybe it's golfers who have given her a bad name. Up and under I had gone, a real Gladys, and then I had come down again.

The ball bobbled about in the heather about fifty yards away.

'A bit of a Gladys, old chap,' said Derrick, the older of our two guests, a smirk on his face, stroking on his ginger sideburns in complacent fashion. We were playing a stableford singles competition in the morning in teams of four, with a rich spread of prizes for the winning guests, but they were nothing compared to the sales orders we were expecting to secure the week following. The morning was the main event, with a greensome for consolation prizes in the afternoon.

'Hard luck,' said the sales director as he made his way on to the tee, his shoulders squared to the task, heavy with confidence.

Come earth and swallow me up, I said to myself. Not a good frame of mind for a round of golf.

Do I have to go through the whole excruciating experience again, hole by horrible hole? Can't you take it as read? Do I have to tell you how my limbs ached with the weary fatigue of abject failure, like Napoleon's shattered men crossing the snow-covered Ukraine on their return from Moscow?

Let me give you an idea. On the third I at least hit a decent tee shot. Such was my enthusiasm that I didn't notice that our to-be-honoured guest, Derrick, was a good twenty yards behind me. I whacked the ball firmly greenward, to hear the shout, 'You've played out of turn, old boy. Just let me play and then you can have another go.'

'That's a bit hard on the boy,' said Tom Swithers, our other guest. He had a dull golf manner, just prodding it up the middle, dull clothes and said little. He meant it kindly, and I was too demoralised to mind being patronised by this nonentity.

'Very well then, Jimbo, let it count,' said Derrick, but Burton determined otherwise.

'Not a hope, strict rules, South.' He laughed. I had no option but to play again.

Naturally I topped my second shot.

Then on the seventh I was just short of the green in two, chipped a little weakly, putted four foot past and missed my return. Four from the edge, a good name for a horse, but yet again I failed to get more than a single stableford point.

And so it continued. Missing my drives into the heather, losing the ball in light rough, and when I did get on the green, three-putting.

As we went round my boss kept up his good humour painfully. 'Hard luck, Jim, you're thinking too hard about the order Derrick's going to give you.'

And Derrick smirked stroking his ginger sideburns, 'I never do business with people who can't beat me at golf.'

The only time Burton's humour slipped was when I moved just before he putted. 'Please keep still, there's a good chap,' he said, adding *sotto voce*, 'that's the least you could do.'

At lunchtime I showered and then took the coward's way out, a double G & T followed by a couple of glasses of white followed by a kümmel. Derrick, rather to my surprise, was in high good spirits, digging me in the ribs and saying I needed to bulk up a bit, while Burton, or David as he now told me I should call him, was recalling with delight how I had addressed the ball on the edge of the bunker on the sixteenth and toppled back into it.

No longer the keen young sales executive, I had become the figure of fun for the party. Even Tom Swithers laughed. It was quite clear to me by this time that my future might be anywhere, but was certainly not in sales.

'Well, once more into the breach,' boomed Derrick. 'Going to show us how to do it this afternoon, then?' – followed by roars of laughter.

I had scored thirteen stableford points in all, the bottom of the table, while Derrick had come second with thirty-seven, not bad out of a field of forty. He would collect a good prize, if not the silver itself.

I was again playing with Derrick in the greensome competition. He was partnering another of my colleagues, and I had been put with a minor client who was not much good either. To be quite honest, I had given up hope as I crept on to the tee.

Funny old game, really. Everything that had gone wrong in the morning went right in the afternoon. The ball fell into the hole from many yards away, my drives hit the fairway at least half the time, and on two occasions the ball bounced back out of the trees into play. It was a joy, and if my hangover hadn't started towards the end, and my partner hadn't buried his bunker shot on the last hole, we would have won the afternoon competition. Derrick was suffering a bit of a hangover, too, it seemed, because he was rather subdued as we walked off the last.

'Well, I really enjoyed that,' I said with real enthusiasm.

'Good,' said Derrick as he strode swiftly off.

Back at the clubhouse we hung around and then at last came the prize-giving. Derrick received his second prize with reasonable grace, but his bonhomie had evaporated. Then we had a few drinks and, as per instructions, I waited until all the clients had left.

As I waited the day came into clearer perspective: I had humiliated my boss in the morning with my incompetence, got drunk at lunch, and then redeemed myself when it no longer mattered.

I sat on the wooden bench in the changing-room and began to ponder other careers. At that moment up walked David Burton, looking decidedly grim.

'Don't ever do that again, not ever, not if you want to go on working for me. Do you understand?'

'I'm sorry, Mr Burton—'

He was not interested in excuses.

'Listen, South, the sort of selfish display you put on today is unforgivable. And I had such hopes for you.'

'I just found it very difficult, sir.'

'Of course you did, we all did, but you managed it perfectly well in the morning. In fact you overdid it, but it was a fault in the right direction. What on earth came over you to ruin Derrick's afternoon?'

I stared down at the wooden floor of the changing-room.

What a lousy boss, a lousy job and a lousy, lousy game.

Silence reigned for a minute or so, and then David Burton said, 'At least you fell in that bunker on the six-teenth,' and left smiling.

Clubs, Choice of

No, not the six-iron across the lake with a slight breeze behind, on to a hard convex green with bunkers beyond, rather than the five you took yesterday when the wind was against and you landed in the drink. No, that's easy. No, I mean the choice of club as the first great hurdle we all face when we realise that golf has entered our bloodstream like an incurable virus.

In my sad case the virus entered under duress. I soon realised that my position with Dave and the sales team was fatally flawed if I couldn't carry on the normal patter: 'What handicap are you?' – 'Nineteen.' – 'Oh, where?' – 'Little Bootling-on-Sea.' – 'Nice course?' – 'Not bad.' – 'Never played it m'self.' – 'Pity, you'd enjoy it. [Pause.] You ought to come down sometime, lovely country.' – 'Oh, thanks, name the day.'

The alternative patter didn't sound so good: 'I play off nineteen.' – 'Where?' – 'Well, I'm down on the waiting list at Old Manor. It's a new course in South Midshire.' – 'Oh, never heard of it.' – 'It's going to be a pretty good course when they finish it.' – 'Be careful with your entrance fee.' – 'You must play on it when they do.' – 'Thanks, but I won't hold my breath.'

So I had to confront the ugly truth: you're not a golfer if you don't have a home club. Or at least you can't be a career golfer, which was all I aspired to. After six months on the sales team, I still woke up in the early hours wreathed in sweat from dreaming I was frozen to the spot, unable to putt from total indecision as to whether to putt to win the match and irritate the client, or to miss from two feet and humiliate myself in front of him.

I threw myself on Dave's mercy.

'I'm enjoying my golf these days,' I said, 'but I've one problem. I'm not a member of a club.'

David's face clouded over, and in his best avuncular manner put his arm round my shoulder.

'You and Groucho Marx, eh?'

It was a crack I would grow familiar with.

Of course, in retrospect I should never have asked him. How would he handle it when he had to sack me in the next recession? My request was like a demand for permanent employment. No wonder his response was so practised.

So I was on my own. I don't know if you've ever studied the habits of the more primitive tribes in the Amazonian interior, though I probably shouldn't call them primitive because they seem only too civilised. But when it comes to creating obligations through providing services and initiating neophytes with horrendous tests of wit and endurance, golf-club joining has it down to a fine art.

I spoke to my father. 'You used to play a bit of golf, Dad. I was thinking of joining a club.'

My father, I remembered, had swung a club in anger for a few years, but he blanched at the implied question.

'Ask your Uncle Jack, he used to be involved in that sort of thing.'

And Uncle Jack gave his usual response.

'Not a bad idea, Jim. I should be able to help. Let's have lunch and talk about it.' You only had to glance at Jack to see lunch played a large part in his life. The broken veins, wisps of hair on his chubby cheeks and his low centre of gravity gave witness to a man who treated himself well after propelling the small white ball into the oncoming storms.

We lunched at a new Italian restaurant of Uncle Jack's choice. After a couple of large vods with tonic, two starters, steak Florentine, a bottle of vintage Chianti and a serious attack on the sweet trolley, he reached the point over his second grappa.

'The basic rules of joining a club apply to golf. Always apply to a club where relatively few people know you, and no one knows you well. Blackballing is one of the few pleasures left to many of us. Seek out a club which needs your subscription. Throw yourself on the mercy of your proposer and seconder, making it quite clear that there is absolutely nothing you want more in the world. Keep away from the club while your name is coming up for selection.

'You may say that these are absurd rules. Everyone knows that a couple of notes to the secretary, three or four to the captain, and a few large ones for another member of the committee and, as the young say, Game Over. But it's not the way for a gentleman to behave.' He looked at me quizzically for a moment before continuing. 'And anyway it's a slippery slope, if you see what I mean.'

I didn't exactly, so I pressed on with my purpose.

'Dad said you were a member somewhere on the south coast. I wondered whether . . .'

'Your esteemed father was thinking of St Wilfrid's. We used to play there as boys, but you wouldn't have a hope of getting in, not an icicle's hope in hell, as the saying goes.' And he laughed rather cruelly.

'Why not?' I asked sharply. I was, after all, paying for lunch.

'Do you have a handicap?'

'No.'

'Well, there you are.' He laughed again.

'Well, how could I have a handicap when I don't belong to a club?'

'Exactly!' he shouted triumphantly. Tears were beginning to run down his cheeks with merriment. 'This tiramisu is really delicious,' he spluttered as he choked with laughter.

'Well, what should I do?' I snarled.

'Join the navy!' he cried and gripped the side of his chair and rocked about, clearly irritating the guests at the next table.

I tried hard to control my anger.

'How did *you* get into St Wilfrid's, Uncle Jack?'

Tears still running down his cheeks, he controlled himself enough to tell me.

'It's an extremely funny story, as a matter of fact. I'll tell you.' He sobered up as he prepared to enthral me with a story entirely about himself.

'Rather like you' – he paused to snigger – 'I became a little over-enthusiastic about golf at one time. And I too discovered it's not that easy to join' – his voice fell an octave – 'a great club.

'Of course in those days the economics were rather different. Our sort of people had been decimated by the war and although there were lots of people who would like to join, there weren't that number of people of the right sort who could afford to join. It was just as bad as not having a handicap.' He began to chortle again.

'So what happened?'

'Well, the club was very strict then. You had to have six signatures, apart from your proposer and seconder. One of them had to be a member of the committee, and all of them,' he added with bated breath, 'had to be current with their subscriptions.'

I gasped dutifully.

'I won't bore you with the blow-by-blow, but it proved hard work. My great-uncle, also called Jack, had put me up, and his playing partner had seconded me, obeying the vital rule.'

'What's that?' I asked naively.

'He had never played with me, of course.'

'And so?' I asked, feigning boredom.

'It all seemed to be going well until the winter turned very cold.'

I looked at him bleakly.

'The wind-chill factor, as they now call it, must have reached minus twenty at the very least, and quite frankly a number of the members simply didn't make it.' He paused and stared dolefully at the table. 'You wouldn't like to get me another grappa?'

'Of course,' I replied, but he had already signalled to the waiter.

'Well, the members can't live for ever, no one expects them to, but that winter took a valuable crop, for amongst them were my fifth and sixth signatures.'

I couldn't help smiling.

'What was I to do? After six months, if you haven't got the signatures . . . *kaput*!' And he ran his finger across his neck.

'They had gone out together on a bright January afternoon. God knows how many kümmels they'd had in the bar. The wind was from the east, which makes the first three holes quite easy. It was the fourth that did for Burrows. He went down the chasm and never came up. Or at least he came up but was then blown down again. Drysdale went to find him and, so it's said, picked him up and tried to continue his round with Burrows on his back. He might have been all right if he hadn't rolled back into the bunker at the seventh. His ball, that is. I think it broke his spirit, for they were found frozen to the ground the next morning. Burrows had been laid down carefully outside the hazard and Drysdale, his face in a ghastly contortion, lay covered in sand, his wedge held in a vice-like grip.'

I began to wonder if Uncle Jack knew where he was.

He sipped his grappa.

'So what was I to do? Time was running out and there wasn't another member who even knew of my existence. Desperate measures were called for. The committee were meeting the next morning.

'It was a full moon as I climbed through the skylight into the members' changing-room. Creeping down the corridor, I made my way into the Members' Bar where the signing-in book lay. I had a blue and a black Biro with me. It was the work of an instant to scribble in the half-light, "Simon Burrows" in blue and "Frederick Drysdale" in black against my name.'

Uncle Jack's face, which had been intense with the memory, now relaxed.

'How did you know their signatures?'

'I didn't,' shouted Uncle Jack, and with the relief of ending the story of personal confession he laughed loudly. 'Just think if after all these years they found I'd got into St Wilfrid's under false pretences!'

I ground my teeth. I had listened to all this rot and

was paying for lunch and I didn't seem any closer to joining a golf club, any club.

I paid, and he regarded the matter as closed.

Nevertheless he had given me, albeit unwittingly, a good piece of advice. Get a handicap first and choose your club later. So I scoured the pages of the golf mags to find somewhere which needed me as much as I needed them. My luck was in: 'Lake Park Country Club, opening soon, new members welcome. Apply Albert Stonegass & Co Ltd.'

I duly filled in the coupon and waited expectantly. Almost by return came some of the glossiest brochures I'd ever seen, but more to the point some extraordinary views of the new course, beautiful tree-lined fairways through lush woodlands. The greens were immaculate; the new clubhouse would have put a Lutyens manor to shame.

The following Saturday saw me en route for Lake Park, a song in my heart.

The telephone call with Albert Stonegass had been slightly disconcerting.

'With a new course like this one, son, you've got to see it as it's going to become, not as it is,' Stonegass had advised me.

I couldn't immediately see how to follow Stonegass's instruction but I gave it a good try, and I was still trying as I strode down the first fairway.

'But it doesn't look much like the fairway in the brochure.'

'Of course it doesn't, that's the fairway of the twelfth.'

'You said you had only completed nine so far.'

'Exactly.'

We walked through the wet grass, the heavy clay sticking to our boots, and Stonegass continued to talk with the sweeping phrase, dropping the household golfing name and spinning a web of the golfing glories that were soon to overcome the farmland. He was a commanding figure, silver hair swept back, his nose somewhat aquiline, and with the bearing of a military man. Air Force, I thought.

'Where's the lake?' I interjected on impulse.

'Glad you asked me that question,' he said and off he went, drawing with great cartwheels in the sky the magnificent series of interlocking water hazards that were planned to separate the ninth and eighteenth in a crescendo of excitement to both nines.

Back in the Nissen hut that acted as a temporary clubhouse, Stonegass moved in for the kill.

'So there you are, Jim. Your golfing days can begin in earnest.'

I was still wavering, but I was more experienced at selling than at buying. My parry was but a poor thing against his thrust, feint and lunge. His next comment caught me off guard.

'You've only got two problems.'

'Oh?' I said.

'First, we need two referees. I'm quite sure you'd be

no trouble to the other members, but I'm sure you understand that we have standards to keep up. The members insist on it.'

'That shouldn't be a problem,' I said with a reasonable degree of confidence.

'They have to be golfing references, you realise.'

'Of course.'

He looked at me carefully, weighing me up, and continued, 'And secondly we require a small deposit in advance.'

'That shouldn't be a problem, either,' I said quickly.

'Good, that's settled, then. Let's get on with the paperwork.'

I dutifully gave him my name, address and telephone numbers for home and office. He then took my work details.

'Is it permanent employment?' he asked.

'I hope so.'

'So do I. Most of our members are prosperous, you understand.'

I nodded. He moved down the page, reached the references, hesitated a moment and then smiled at me.

'We'll take those up later. All you need do now is sign up and I'll get it processed.'

'Isn't there a joining fee?' I asked naively. Uncle Jack had warned me about them.

'No, not exactly. We call it a deposit, but it comes to the same thing.'

'Oh, fine. What's the damage?'

'We've managed to keep it down to one year's membership. Normally we require both the deposit and first year's subscription at signing-up, but as you probably remember from the magazine we have a special offer on until the first ball is struck.'

He pushed the form across to me.

'Congratulations on becoming a founder member of Lake Park Golf and Country Club.'

Before I could sign he shook my hand vigorously. At last I took up the Biro again and signed my name. I might as well have carved it.

'If you just give me a cheque for the deposit I'll get it processed.'

It only then occurred to me I hadn't taken in one detail.

'How much?'

'Oh, didn't I tell you?' He laughed. 'Six hundred pounds, plus VAT. Excellent value.'

I have to say I hesitated, but not long enough. This was an historic step for me towards a lofty goal, the Elysian fields complete with eighteen flags, tee boxes, bunkers and 'ground under repair' signs.

I took out my cheque book and with never another word signed.

My heart was heavy with anticlimax as I drove back to London, but over the following weeks it rose again with a brief flutter when news of Lake Park arrived: 'Course on track for June opening. World class bunkers in place round the eighth green.'

By late May I couldn't wait to get down there. Still I controlled myself and arrived early on a dank cold morning typical of the beginning of June.

I was not alone at Lake Park that morning. The car park was full of the widest selection of motors you'd ever hope to lay eyes on, and the crowd itself was equally varied. It came to me quickly, however, that the crowd of over a hundred people was united by a common enthusiasm. No, not to pace the verdant swathe between the noble oaks of the new, great course. This would have been difficult because if anything the farmland looked even less like a golf course than it had four months earlier. No, the enthusiasm was to find Albert Stonegass and show him in unspeakable ways other uses for golf clubs and golf balls. Indeed the crowd was growing ugly, so that each new arrival had to prove that they had no personal knowledge of, nor association with, A. Stonegass Esquire, golf-course maker to nobody. One man, slower on the uptake, seemed to take a friendly view of Stonegass and very nearly had his car turned over.

Back at my flat I sat in deep depression. I thought of my mates at work to whom I had boasted of my new club, and I slipped deeper into gloom. I thought long and hard; something was suggesting itself to me. At last I picked up the telephone.

'Is that you, Uncle Jack?'

'Of course it is, Jim. Always nice to hear you.'

'Thanks, Uncle Jack, but to get straight to the point, I need your help.'

'Always delighted to help, Jim. What about a spot of lunch? That Italian restaurant was awfully good.'

'No, I don't think that will be necessary. You see, Uncle, all I want you to do is to put me up for St Wilfrid's.'

Jack started to laugh.

'Join the navy, I told you . . .'

I interrupted him.

'Jack, let's stop fooling about. I want you to get me into St Wilfrid's. It's very simple. Either we're both members or neither of us is.' I was desperate. Uncle Jack was the only way.

'What's got into you, Jim? Have you been drinking?'

'You know what I mean, Jack. Those signatures, your signatures, the blue and black ones, remember?'

There was a silence the other end. Then bluster: 'Don't be so foolish, young man.' Then false humour: 'It was only a joke, Jim, we'd had a good lunch.' Finally he whined, 'I don't know who will sign for you, it's a long waiting list.'

'You'll find a way, Jack, you usually do.' And then I added, perhaps unkindly, 'You can always invite them to lunch.'

Well, needs must when the devil rides, and though there was a bit of a waiting list, and Uncle Jack moaned off and on over the next eighteen months, the glorious day arrived. As a little joke I signed my entry form and cheques in different coloured inks.

Golf Incorporate

I was looking forward with keen anticipation to the corporate day. No more the hopping furry friend; now the feral beast stalking the verdant turf. No more self-doubt; or anyway, not much – and then only in especially tense moments. No, I was the master of my game, untouchable by human kind.

These very positive thoughts are exactly the right sort to carry you through most golfing experiences, even corporate days, were it not for the intervention of that lowest of human instincts. I refer not to the will to win, nor even the wish to lose on purpose, but – lowest of all – the escapism of not caring who wins.

'Of course it doesn't matter if you win, Jim, just make sure they enjoy themselves,' said David Burton, in his heavy manner.

'But last year you chewed me out for playing too well.'

'It wasn't that you played too well; you didn't, particularly.' Note the mean spirit typical of certain golfers. 'It was that you were only interested in your own game.'

'It was a wonder I was interested in anything after all that kümmel.'

'I'll come to the kümmel later. As I was saying, a corporate day is a chance for a good day out in friendly circs, letting the sunny side of your character show.'

'Do you expect that? On a golf course?'

'I expect you to be more interested in your guest's game than in your own. If you win, that's your affair, and if you play good golf your guests will probably forgive you, though you won't actually win any prizes, of course – they're for the guests. Anyway, your own game is the least of your worries.'

Dave Burton, sales director 'sans pareil', that is 'without equal' to those of you lucky enough to be unburdened by the lingo of the gallant Gaul, was really getting up my nose. He still treated me like an errant spaniel, even though he knew my figures were the best of the region for the first half. 'Seen my figures?' I'd said to him earlier in the week and he'd just humphed, implying there might be some doubt about them. I had a nasty feeling about it.

It has to be said that the relations between a salesman and his director are rather like those between a club golfer and his pro – an uneasy mutual dependency. Whatever progress the clubman makes, he knows he will still be regarded with pity verging on contempt, even though the pro is dependent on his striving pupil for his livelihood. And, as we all know, the sales director lives off the back of his salesmen. Bitter, do you say? Well, you've obviously not spent the winter months in the maw of a set of golf lessons, but let it pass.

'And enjoy the kümmel by all means, but don't forget what the day is for.'

'Golf?'

'Don't irritate me, Jim.'

I arrived promptly at the chosen venue, as for last year set in the forbidding pines and heather of Surrey, in more than good time. Living in digs not far from the offices of the agency, located in part of the Southern development beneath the M25, I was given to a few beers in the local with some of the other fellows from the pit face, as we called it, before turning in early enough to ensure a fresh start.

On this particular morning I had woken with a start and looked at my alarm clock. 7:25. Jeez! I thought. That wally Burton would be a real pain if I wasn't there before my partner for the morning. I had been assigned Ray Ostles, finance director of Ostles and Co., a local contractor which we were very keen to see on our books. He was a hammered-down little man who had seen better days but still had a big cheque book. Burton's parting shot from the day before had been, 'We want access, do you understand?'

Anyway, I was out of the house like a jack-rabbit and fetched up at the club slightly panicked in what I thought was adequate time. I had had a lucky run on the M25 and was even more surprised to find the club car park empty. The situation became more apparent when I examined the hands of my watch more closely to see it was only 6:35. I realised I'd mistaken 5:35 for 7:25, an easy enough mistake to make with the elegant traditional hands of my alarm clock rather than green neon blinking at me with its digital-doos. This morning the price of elegance seemed rather high.

I felt a bit of a moron as I sloped round the clubhouse trying to see if any staff had arrived who could give me a cup of coffee. I suppose the sensible thing would have been to wait, but I knew a little café not far off back on the M25.

So life took its pre-appointed course. It's funny how those roads fill up between 7:37 AM and 7:39 AM, and how short cuts round the back can be awfully beguiling, but anyway things were fairly buzzing by the time I got back to the clubhouse, my stomach an uneasy mixture of grapefruit juice, coffee, bacon, sausage, black pudding, fried egg on fried toast, coffee, marmalade on toast, coffee and so on.

'Where the hell have you been?' hissed Burton like a demented porcupine.

I thought it undignified to explain in detail.

'Trouble with the watch.'

'You'll have trouble somewhere else if you're not over to the tee in ten seconds flat. Ray Ostles is in an ugly mood.' That figures, I thought to myself. 'And he so enjoys a game with his account executive, you'll see,' added Burton with what I took to be malice.

Ray Ostles was about the most boring golfer I'd ever played with. Even when he hooked it out of bounds it just dribbled through the fence.

'Hard luck, Ray, I'm afraid it'll just have reached the white posts.'

'We'll see when we get there, won't we,' said Ostles in a monotone.

He saw when he got there, while I was looking for my ball in the light rough on the right. The next thing I knew, his ball was speeding up the hill and up the fairway.

'You got lucky, then,' I said when we reached the green at the top of the hill.

'Of course I did,' he replied in that tone of voice which might have added, *you berk*!

Anyway, he plugged along for his five with a boring pitch, a boring approach putt and a boring stab to put it away.

'Solid start, Ray.'

'You think so?'

No, he didn't say – 'Thank you Jim, nice of you to say so' – just a curt interrogative.

I don't think people can be so rude unless they think there's some convention involved. You're the host, they're the guest, and it's your job to keep them happy however obnoxious they are, because you've invited them as rather a crude piece of selling effort. A cynical view? Definitely, but unfortunately shared by Dave Burton and Ray Ostles.

'Let's inject a bit of friendly competition into it, shall we?' suggested Ostles, as he prepared to tee off across the heather and over the hill to a green over 440 yards away.

'If you like.' I had an inkling of what was to come.

'Chicago, okay? Ten, ten and twenty,' he barked at me like a stunted terrier.

'That's fine.' I've never seen the point of gambling on the golf course, it's agony at a double price, except the agony is without price and victory needs no sweetening. Chicago is particularly uncalled for as you can lose three times over, front nine, back nine and the match. Ostles was clearly a sadist to boot.

'Not too much money, I hope?'

'I can manage,' I said, trying not to sound proud. It was too much money, really, especially on a salesman's salary. Ostles must have known it. He must also have known that a few placements from him and I'd have been laughing. What a hope!

Anyway, the game and Ostles continued in this crass vein until we got to the fourth. He had played bogey golf, no reference to his nose which he dug around in sporadically, and I was on the elevated green in two. He had hit a big drive, with his big head special, and had gone behind a tree. Actually not just a tree but a bit of choice heather and old leaves into the bargain. No hope! I had thought to myself with mild pleasure. My feet had swelled and I bent down to tie my shoelaces a little looser, if you know what I mean, and I looked across out of the corner of my eye into the woodland where the guest was rootling.

There's a sort of surreptitious lurch which I've seen

before which Ray made now. I fixed my gaze on him. He scrabbled like a mongrel in the leaves behind the tree, then stood sharply up. When he adjusted his cardigan and took some practice swings the ball was in the clear. He hacked it on without difficulty.

'Had some difficulty in there?' I enquired politely.

'Caught short, old man. It's the age.'

'Oh,' I said with a suppressed sneer.

At the sixth the mood momentarily lightened, when he hooked the ball under the trees to the left. I hit rather a good four iron, the ball bouncing gently across the grass ditch in front of the green, to be on in two, and I put my putt dead for a solid par.

'Good work, young man,' said the patronising sod, but anyway we were all square to the ninth.

The ninth is burned into my memory. Yet again he hooked it and this time I knew I was home free. Unbeknownst to those who have not been grilled on the cold pines of this particular Nordic torture, to be perhaps a little cruel to this great course, the ninth boasts a large but hidden lake to the left. You'd better get your water-wings on, I mused with satisfaction.

'In the lake, I'm afraid,' I ventured.

'You don't say,' he replied nonchalantly.

We strolled down the hill, a downward swoop which then rolled up again to the green just below the clubhouse. To spoil my good humour, I saw the yellow-clad figure of Burton with heavy but rapid tread coming down towards us from the clubhouse. Like the knowledgeable golfer he wasn't, he remained quiet until close enough to speak in a stage whisper.

'Putting our young friend to the sword, eh, Ray?'

'He's fighting well, David, fighting well.'

'Like a trout, Ray, eh?'

'What's that?'

'Like a trout.'

'Oh.' He paused, nonplussed. 'I wouldn't be surprised.'

'Ray's in the drink, I'm afraid to say,' I chipped in brightly.

'We'll see about that,' said Burton harshly and shot off towards the lake like a frenzied bulldog, Ray sloping off after him, his shoulders hunched in an encouraging manner.

'Just short of the lake!' cried out Burton.

'Well, that's a piece of luck,' said Ostles, genuinely surprised.

When we got to the green the two were smiling happily.

'You must have found a golfing trout,' I said.

'How's that?' said Burton. He looked mean and ugly and I bit my tongue.

The fact of the matter was that I now had Ostles sized up. He was one of those golfing asses who actually wants a lower handicap than they can really handle, not that I don't sympathise. Standing in the bar and saying something like, 'I'm off twenty-six, actually,' can't be a load of laughs, anyway not for the teller of the tale. In Ostles's case twenty-two would have been about right, but he insisted on showing off off fifteen. Served him right, really. Anyway, I knew he would lose to me if some larger force didn't intervene.

'I thought you were pretty lucky to find Ray's ball in the lake.'

Ray was polishing his putter head by his trolley so he didn't catch this remark, or its irony.

Burton walked over to me, a certain fierceness in his eye, took me by the crook of my arm and despite his diminutive size virtually frog-marched me over to the other side of the green.

'Listen, wise guy.' I really hate these pseudo-American efforts at slang. 'Ray Ostles asked to play with you because he wants to get a relationship going, get things moving, give you some commission, you creep. Be nice to him, okay?'

I suppose one ought to keep one's sense of proportion, even one's sense of humour, on such occasions, but instead I used a four-letter word or two and shook Burton off, returning to my putt.

The ninth at Darkley Wood has a pig of a green, and although we were both on for three neither achieved a bogey. Ostles slapped me on the back and said with charmless good humour, 'Well, it's forty on the second nine.'

Forty quid is serious money, in anybody's language,

but I was confident but for one niggling thought. Could I rely on Ostles not to cheat? Okay, I've said it. That was the thought that was running through my mind, and there's no more destructive thought to a round of golf.

On the tenth I was just short in two. Ostles got stuck in the heather ridge fifty yards short and I thought he was dead. Somehow he hacked out on to the edge and rolled up to four feet and we halved it. How come he was so lucky with his lie?

'I was lucky with my lie in the heather,' said a jovial Ostles.

I grunted. It was under my skin. He couldn't go into the rough without me sidling over to see how he lay.

'Don't worry, young man,' he said to me on the fifteenth, 'it's sitting up fine.'

'Fine,' I echoed, walking quickly off to my ball. It was becoming obsessional, an unhealthy suspicion, especially so since I couldn't determine what to do if or when I caught him in the act.

My game suffered and we came to the last all square. It was of course a stableford competition, but we had both lost all interest in that. It was the forty pounds, and the glory of victory over the big account, that held my attention.

To my dismay, as we crested the hill – or rather shoulder – that guarded the direct approach to the eighteenth, I saw once more the square yellow-clad figure of Burton bowling towards us. I had hit a peach and had an easy pitch on to the green. Ostles was halfway up the shoulder and had to hit a difficult ball across the second valley on to the green. He took a five-iron, got under it and lodged in the heather thirty yards short, still with an uphill lie. I pitched on, but the green is sharp and sloping and I ended off to the bottom left, almost rolling into the bunker.

What happened then still grates. I walked to the top left-hand side of the green to put down my clubs, and to take a position where I could just see over the ridge to where Ostles was about to play. Then it happened. As Ostles addressed the ball it rolled back about two inches. Actually I felt quite sorry for him at first, but then a second thought came into my head. The bastard, I thought. At that moment a hand landed on my shoulder.

'How's it going? Ray had a good round?' said Burton.

'He's just cheated.'

'What?' spluttered Burton.

'I said, he's just cheated. You probably saw it.'

'Listen, even if he has, which I don't believe, don't say a word.'

'He's playing for forty quid and he's cheated. In fact,' I added with a voice like cold steel, 'he's cheated all the way round and now I've caught him.'

At that moment there was a thud and Ostles's ball landed on the green and rolled six feet past the hole.

I began to move down to play my ball, but Burton

held me by the arm. 'If you say a word about cheating, you're fired. Fired, got it?'

I shook myself free, strode to my ball and chipped it up. I was shaking and I jerked the club head, skulling it ten feet past.

Ostles was standing below the green. He left his trolley and stood on the other side of the hole. Burton was gritting his teeth, his knuckles white, locked in indecision.

I stood over the ball. It was a downhill curling putt. If I missed it I had decided to accuse the bastard of cheating. My mind was made up.

'What's the problem, son?' Ostles interrupted my concentration. I looked up.

'What do you mean?' I asked.

'I had a penalty shot in the heather. I've played four,' he said in a nonchalant way. Did he realise what he had put me through?

The sun came through the clouds and the beauty of the rhododendron-lined course revealed itself to me. No need to tell the bastard he'd cheated, no danger for the forty quid. I stroked the ball up and it stopped a few inches short, but I had a safe five.

'Well, I've got this to save,' said Ostles with surprising good humour. Across the sloping green he didn't have a chance, and the money was mine.

'Good game, Jim. Went to the last. Could've gone either way,' said Ostles, slapping his arm round my shoulder. 'Let's go and have a pre-lunch snifter.'

I realised at that moment that Ray Ostles was not such a bad sort at all, and he was right: it had been a good contest.

It was only the next morning that the birds came home to roost.

'Pack your things and get out by ten, Jim.'

'What?' I said, genuinely perplexed.

'You heard. You're fired.'

'But you can't.' I paused, working it out quickly. 'Anyway, Ostles said he was going to take a twelve-week slot.'

'Get real, Jim. You know what happened.'

'We had a friendly game of golf, that's all.'

'Listen, Jim,' – sorrow was beginning to replace anger – 'don't you realise, selling has to come before golf in all circumstances, especially extreme ones. Nothing else is possible, for a salesman, that is.'

I was stunned. 'You can't mean it.'

He put his hand on my shoulder and I realised that he did. In the deepening gloom, as I realised what it meant to lose my job, I could nevertheless hear the trumpets of the great golfing ideal beckoning me into a better world.

'Why don't you become a solicitor, an accountant, a doctor, even a lion-tamer? A good solid professional job. Then at least you can put your golf first.'

It wasn't bad advice.

The Will to Win

'Listen, Doug, what matters is the will to win. Either you choke or you don't.'

I thought I was making a rather obvious point.

'You're forgetting the basic skill level, Jim. If you're a good golfer, that's what you are. Sometimes you'll play your best game when you really need to. Other times you won't.'

'That's what I mean – it's psychology. You've either got it or you haven't.'

'Maybe, Jim, but I'd say luck plays a much bigger part.' He paused and then, with a certain amount of condescension, continued. 'Take my putt on the seventeenth which, let's face it, wrapped it up for me. A ten-footer across the slope. Maybe I'll sink it three times in ten. I was lucky; you were unlucky.'

It was the sort of comment golfers like to make after a game. It reminds their opponent of a particularly galling moment under the pretence of an interesting or useful comment, often with an undertow of false modesty, the only sort of which golfers have any experience.

None the less, it was a well-made point. I had been unlucky to lose, and I stared into the lager a moment as we sat in the clubhouse after the game. How should I put it?

'Look, Doug, I don't want to be insulting, but you

47

sank that putt because it didn't really matter. It doesn't make that much difference to either of us who wins a friendly.' This was more or less true, probably less. 'But the point is, who would've won if something turned on it?'

Doug gave me quite a cold look with his pale blue eyes, a slight frown with his mouth turned down, then raised his eyebrows, drew on his pint and said easily, 'Well, we'll have a chance to find out. We've drawn each other in the first round of the Captain's Cup. The draw's just gone up.'

The Captain's Cup, the annual club tournament that really mattered; he was right, it would test our will to win. 'Well, that's a coincidence. No more Mr Nice Guy!'

'Well, that's true for both of us.' He looked at my empty glass, wiped the froth from his thin brown moustache and asked, 'Like another one, Jim?'

I had finished the pint and looked at my watch. 'No, I don't think so. I've promised to take Sammy out and I must get back and shower.'

'You better had. She's a lovely girl – I can't think what she sees in you.'

'Will to win, old chap.'

'Luck!'

I had met Sammy at a party given by someone I worked with. She had been going out with the same chap for a few years, but his job had taken him out to Sydney,

Australia and she was not sure she wanted to follow. She was completing her accountancy qualifications and had the chance to carry on with Cluttle and Brown, probably the best provincial accountants around our neck of the woods.

She was not only smart, in the American sense, she was pretty and fun, with freckles and chestnut hair, the pick of English womanhood, and I fell for her. And she did for me.

After that first meeting we settled into a steady pattern – dinner on Saturday night and some leisurely tennis on Sunday morning down at the club. She was a big girl with long legs, a definite asset in most circumstances, especially mixed doubles. Saturday I kept for golf.

Doug was not alone in taking a shine to Sammy, but I was the man in possession and meant to keep it that way.

Dinner with Sammy was in many ways the high point of my week, made even better if I'd had a couple of good rounds on Saturday. Not so hot if I hadn't, but still fun, relaxing, perhaps too relaxing.

'You don't think we're getting into a bit of a rut, Jim? Every Saturday night like this?'

'Good heavens, no! Or at least' – and I may have smirked – 'a jolly pleasant rut.'

'Couldn't we do something different occasionally?' She was looking at me rather hard. 'Like go out for lunch on Saturday, or something daring like that?'

In my experience women do not have much sense of irony, so I felt sure she had something specific in mind.

'Why Saturday lunch, Foxy?' I used my favourite name for giving her a little tease; after all, she knew Saturday was my golf day.

She continued, quite refusing to rise, 'Well, there's a steam fair at Hyde and we could have a picnic and a walk along Mallory Cliffs.'

'Sounds lovely, darling.' Then a thought struck me. If I were to lose to Doug, I would for once in the year only play eighteen holes on Saturday, and be free for Saturday afternoon.

'All right, Sammy, we'll do it if I lose in the Captain's Cup on Saturday morning.'

'Well, mind you lose.' She put her hand in mine, but I thought her voice had an edge to it.

Saturday morning was wet and windy. A southwesterly blew across the bay to St Wilfrid's and the forecast was for showers, but with the wind moderating and a sunny afternoon.

We were to tee off at 8:47 AM. As usual I was there an hour beforehand to hit a few practice balls and sharpen up my putting. I have to admit the thought had crossed my mind that, even if I lost, the second prize, an afternoon with Sammy, was not too shabby. But I'm pretty sure it didn't impair my will to destroy Doug in the Captain's Cup.

Doug arrived at the tee at 8:40, looking cheerful and relaxed, a glint in his eye.

'Well, Jim, I'm going to trust to luck, and you to your will to win. Call!'

'Heads!'

'Heads it is. Your honour.'

The game really went in two phases. To begin with, I hit the ball rather well. On the 520 yards par five, the first, I was about forty yards short in two. Doug sliced his first into the light rough on the bank on the right, thinned his recovery and had about 180 yards to the green. He faded one off to the right and put his chip twenty feet past. I was putting for a birdie from about eight feet. His long putt curled round the hole and dropped in for par. Slightly irritated, I missed the eight-footer.

You see what I mean? Good recovery play, or the will to win? To me it was obvious. Doug had hit his long putt with a carefree swing and had stroked it in. When the pressure was on, the twitching would start.

I have to admit that by the turn his nonchalance was beginning to get to me. He had sunk another couple of putts of over ten feet and had chipped dead from tough lies on two more occasions. My game was much steadier but I just could not finish properly. The fact was, I was three down at the turn.

Then something happened. I have to say that I tight-ened my game a notch, but as we chatted away I saw his imperturbability begin to leave him and he started to play like a man wrestling with some personal devil. Strangely enough his long game held together, but his short game was suffering from appalling indecision.

I won the tenth, which helped, Doug missing from six feet. But he won the eleventh with a brilliant recovery from the bunker, short of the green to the right, with a nasty high face. He dug down on the ball and up it popped to within three feet.

So it went on, with him duffing chips one hole, sinking fifteen-footers the next. As we came to the seventeenth, he was still one up but I felt I was in with a chance. My tail was up.

It's a long par three with a track running across diagonally upwards from left to right. The green slopes downwards from the track with a ridge on the other side of it, in which a line of pot bunkers stand.

As so often with links courses, the easy way to play it is short. Leave the ball on the track to the right and roll up the second to within a few feet for a safe par. The green is curvaceous, but play it a few times and it has no terrors.

Any full-length ball hit to the left, or even straight if it gets the slope wrong, will end in the pot bunkers, leaving a horrible explosion shot.

It was my honour and my blood was up. I decided to take a three wood and put it to the flag, the full 225 yards. As I stood at the tee I thought fleetingly about the afternoon with Sammy. Yes, the merest idling moment of less than full dedication and the ball went off with enough draw to find the last of the pot bunkers.

I gritted my teeth as Doug walked past me, but his face was equally grim. None the less he played the percentage ball well, a fading three-iron, leaving him with a reasonable running chip. He could equally well putt.

I exploded out well but rolled past the hole at least fifteen feet. Doug putted up to six feet. I missed. He had the six-footer to win.

I'll never forget his face full of grim intent as he walked up to take the putt. He looked like a man in terrible agony, perhaps excruciating stomach cramp or worse. He studied the putt from every angle, from above, below, from both sides. He took four practice swings. He was almost a caricature of a man trying to sink a crucial putt. He winced as he hit.

As I've said, the greens are tremendously fast at St Wilfrid's and his putt was slightly downhill, always more difficult than clearly downhill. Anyway the ball just crept up to the hole, saluted to the right and crept on by, and on and on. It stopped about six feet past. He stood there watching like a disconsolate traveller who sees the last train pull out.

He straightened his back and, without a show of irritation, walked up to his ball. He looked almost relieved for, with none of the earlier preparation, he stroked the ball smoothly up to the hole. This time he was about a foot short. He shrugged.

On the eighteenth he sliced his drive into the thorn bushes. We were all square and I had put mine well down the middle, on what everyone will agree is a pig of a final hole.

'I'll play a provisional.'

'Just as well.'

He sliced his provisional into much the same thorn bush. We found that, but it was unplayable. He did not find his first.

'Well played, Jim,' he said as we shook hands amongst the thorns. 'You came back well.' He seemed to be taking it very well.

'You were unlucky at the end, Doug.' I did not allude to my superior determination.

'Oh, I don't know. You were the better man on the day. Perhaps you did have a greater will to win.' He smiled quite genuinely.

I almost replied, 'Not really, old chap, you had the will to lose,' but I thought it would be ungallant.

'Let's have a drink anyway,' I offered.

Then he did surprise me.

'I don't really feel like it. Do you mind, in the circumstances?' It was the first time he had ever refused a drink, and he had lost to me before, even if not in quite such an important match.

'Of course not, old chap.'

'Best of luck with the next round.' With that he hoisted up his bag and strode off. I felt sorry for him for a moment, but then I thought that perhaps he was not being a very good loser. I would have to recount my victory in the bar myself. Still, he had lost, and I felt a victor's condescension as I saw him drive off in his open-topped black BMW.

Back in the clubhouse, I made my way to the bar.

'Good round, Jim?' Asked Bob, through the tobacco smoke.

'Yes, thanks, Bob.'

'Put Doug to the sword?'

'Well, I did, actually,' and I began to re-live the round. Bob listened politely enough for at least a hole and then I showered.

Only when I reached the bar again did I remember Sammy.

'Hold on, Harry, I must just give someone a call.' Harry laughed.

I've never much enjoyed talking to answer machines, but I calculated that she must have found some other way to get to the steam fair.

I have to say that at this point luck did seem to play a part. To put it simply, I found three bunkers on the outward nine. I was still in with a chance but found a particularly ugly divot on the seventeenth and my opponent fluked a birdie. In other words, I lost.

But that was only the beginning of my bad luck.

I went round as per normal to see Sammy that evening but she was still out. I rang at eleven and the answerphone replied. I thought of going round to see her but then, I said to myself, it was her prerogative. Still, I worried about her.

After watching a little more TV, I decided to call her friend Sarah.

'You didn't see Sammy at the steam fair, did you, Sarah?'

'Oh, Jim, it's you.'

'Yes. I was playing golf. I couldn't make it to the fair. I just hope Sammy did.' I felt a bit unnatural.

'Oh, yes.' She waited for a moment and I wondered whether to ask, 'Who with?'

Unprompted, she continued, 'She was there with some of the gang from Cuttle and Brown.'

'Oh, good.' Perhaps she was aware I had a hidden agenda. 'You see, the thing is, Sarah, she doesn't seem to be back yet.'

'I wouldn't worry. She's probably home and asleep. She's a big girl, Jim.'

'Of course. Well, thanks a lot, Sarah. See you soon. 'Bye.'

''Bye.'

I suppose I really knew then, but I only found out for sure the next weekend. The first pointer was when Doug cancelled our Saturday golf date, but I did not twig then. Nor when Sammy said she would like to meet me at the restaurant on Saturday evening.

She arrived looking extra beautiful and a bit ashen. She turned her cheek as I kissed her. By then I knew the main message. I felt cold inside, rather like when you've left your tee shot short at the seventh and you see the ball rolling back off the green into the deep, deep bunker below.

'Sit down, Jim.'

'What's the matter, Sammy?' But I knew the answer.

'I've found someone else.'

'Who?'

She looked down at her hands. 'Doug.'

'Doug!' I went from shock to anger. 'Doug!' To eventual resignation. 'Doug!' It was a triplicate of emotions I would ride for the next few days.

She saw how shocked I was. 'I'm sorry, Jim, it just happened.'

She seemed genuinely sorry. I gritted my teeth. I had to fight back. Maybe I was dormie four down, but you have never lost until you lose.

'Well, let's at least have dinner. Talk it over. You know how much fun we have together. No point in wasting an evening.'

'No, Jim, I can't. Doug's coming here to pick me up in about twenty minutes.'

I recognised the authentic slamming of the door. She

looked at me sadly, even more sadly than before, and proceeded to lock the slammed door.

'You know, it was your fault, Jim.'

'What on earth do you mean?' I was angry now.

'Well, you shouldn't have told Doug you were taking me out last Saturday afternoon. That is, you were taking me out if you lost.'

I had no recollection of telling Doug that, but I supposed I might have said something of the sort to ease the tension. I thought rapidly as to what I could reply but the knife was in and she twisted it.

'And, Jim, when it came to it, you put a game of golf above me. I quite understand that, but Doug took a different view. He put an afternoon with me first.'

I was dumbfounded. I was truly flabbergasted. And the worst of it only came to me later, after Doug and Sammy had left. Doug would always be able to say he lost on purpose. Not that many golfers would believe him.

Learning My Lesson

There was a song in my heart as I carried my handful of clubs down the swinging bays of the driving range towards a free slot. Gone was the gloom which had lowered my spirits for a week or so after the demise of my relationship with Sammy. The sun was shining, the weekend stretched ahead of me, and it was going to be golf, golf, golf. Who needs a woman when you've got golf! I somewhat naively thought.

As I strolled along, a light swagger in my step, I idly noted the appalling swings of my fellow practitioners on that shining day. There was the crouched gorilla, gripping his club with ferocious concentration, knees crooked, shoulders hunched, and the swing about to be unleashed of a demonic fury which would wrench the ball fifty yards or so to the extreme left of the range. I waited and was only slightly disappointed to see the battered, striped pill skew off to the right.

Then there was the beanpole, standing like the stanchion of a hop field, everything straight and rigid, and when the time came to hit the ball an extraordinary slowness pervaded the movement, like an action replay. The ball looped forward, straight, but a very short way. I was intrigued to see beanpole repeat the performance with apparent satisfaction.

Of course there were players who hit the ball with fluidity and grace, but I didn't spend much time looking at them, smugly conscious that a word or two from me could have ironed out their incipient slice or hook. You see, I had spent the evenings of the preceding week studying something Sammy had given me as a farewell present: a book called *Put the Swing First*.

I also ambled on past the number of young women, some of them quite stylish, who were hitting the ball with the concentration of the gorilla but with even less effect than the beanpole. I have to say the thought crossed my mind that they would have been better employed on a tennis court, or perhaps beside a swimming-pool, not to say at a decent shopping centre.

The visit to the range was the first step in my weekend campaign to show Dai, with whom I shared a flat, who was boss on the course. I had with me a driver, a three-iron, a six and a nine, and my plan was to play the changes, to concentrate on each shot as though I was on the course, and to hone out the little wrinkles that sometimes interfered with perfection.

There is no greater fall from grace than the fall of the conceited golfer. You only have to play idly with the possibility that you've mastered some aspect of the self-inflicted torture called golf, than an awful Nemesis follows. So it was that morning.

Today I know that the most any of us can hope for is periods of remission from the horrors of the slice, top,

sky, hook, push, pull, brought on by the merest imper-
fection in address, grip, shoulder-plane position, weight
shift, ankle turn, wrist cock, head movement, to name
but a sprinkling of the necessary considerations. Be
thankful for the periods of remission, I say; failure is all
we can hope for. But this comforting wisdom had not yet
been vouchsafed me that March morning.

'Practice makes perfect' was my hope when I took to
the driving range. After five drives I was confirmed in my
absolute confidence. The sixth drive revealed a develop-
ing slice. I shifted to the three-iron and thinned it
straightish; the seventh I topped. The eighth was skied
off the rubber tee, the ninth I played off the mat and
thinned it again. I took the nine-iron to restore my
rapidly declining confidence and hit a beauty. I returned
to the driver and had a period of remission but, for fear
of losing the rhythm, I began to play quicker and
quicker, choosing to ignore the shots that went agley
and forgetting all the precepts carefully learned from
the book during the week. I had concluded after a while
that they were in any case all quite useless. By the time I
was through my third basket I was in despair.

The sun had gone in by the time I left the range and I
drove disconsolately back to the flat. Over a cup of
midday Nescafé, I put it to Dai: 'Why does Arnold
Palmer get luckier the more he practises and I get worse?'

'Because you're practising your errors, getting rather
good at them in fact,' smirked Dai. Dai, the son of an

Irish father and Welsh mother, was never short of helpful insights. 'What you need is a lesson.'

These are fateful words, which the experienced golfer regards with the sort of trepidation that actors have for the Scottish play. Now if people suggest I should have a lesson I have the same sort of reaction as when people tell me I should cut out bread during lunch or a G & T before supper, not that I've anything against either idea, in fact I know I'm susceptible to good resolutions. What I do is take a nice long walk until they've worn off.

But if you've had a morning at the range and your hands are raw and your feet are sore, and you've got a big game tomorrow and you've learned nothing, well, exasperation sets in. Any idea, however bad, will be listened to, even one from your flatmate. I knew a chap who believed all he needed to do was rub his chest with embrocation before he played, to loosen up the muscles to a steady level. Of course this sort of thing is sympathetic magic, auto-suggestion and such like, and works wonderfully until it fails, which it always does. One bad round and it's back to the drawing-board – the drawing-room might be a better idea.

So, 'What you need is a lesson,' was Dai's advice. A shudder ran down my back. I'm not superstitious, though in retrospect I have good reason to be. No, I suspect it was the thought of allowing another human being into the private grief which had become, in one short morning, my golf game.

So I called the pro. A Scot of infinite patience but few words, he was slow to come to the phone.

'Andy, it's Jim South. I'm very sorry to give you so little notice but I just must have a lesson before tomorrow.' Pause. 'I've a game against Dai O'Neill and I don't want to let him down. By not beating him, that is.' Pause. 'Not that there's anything fundamentally wrong with my game; just a bit of tightening up is all that's needed. If you see what I mean.'

Andy listened to my babble in silence.

'You want a lesson, do you?'

'Well, if there's any chance. I know it's short notice.'

'No chance.'

'Oh.' I was crestfallen. A silence ensued.

'Would you like to book a lesson? I have a time available next Saturday.'

'Well, yes,' I said without much conviction. I felt somewhat cheated. Like with a visit to the dentist, I had summoned up the nerve to go and now I had to wait a full week for the horror of it.

'Nine o'clock?' he asked in a tone of command.

I resisted the temptation to say it was a bit early, fearing Andy's contempt for late risers.

'That'll be great.' Then I summoned up more courage. 'You wouldn't be able just to look at my swing this afternoon, if you're down on the practice ground anyway?'

This impertinence was followed by a very long silence.

'I'll be down there around tea-time,' he said, without any very clear commitment.

When I drove up to the practice ground around 4:30 I was glad to see Andy there. He had a rather pleasant young woman under instruction, who was hitting what looked like a six-iron straight but obviously not very far.

I watched from a distance. Poor girl, I thought. However hard she practises she'll never feel the joy of the drive soaring down the fairway, 250 yards from the tee. No man would play golf if it wasn't for the drive, I thought; it was like bonfire night without fireworks.

She smiled shyly as she left Andy, who to my mind had rather short-changed her. From what I could see the last ten minutes of her lesson had been a long monologue from the suddenly loquacious Scot. He should have been watching her hit balls, I mused. I had certainly enjoyed watching her. She made a heart-warming sight, her cheeks flushed, her hair sensibly tied-up in a pony-tail, and her brows knit in concentration on Andy's words, a real golfer's woman.

'I'd forgotten about you,' he said as I walked up.

'Oh, I'm sorry,' I said. 'Would you like to leave it, then?'

'No, I'll have a look at you. Get out your five-iron.'

I did as he asked and took up my stance. He walked around me slowly and sniffed.

'Take a few practice swings.'

Self-consciously I swung the club around a few times and then stopped.

'A few more, please, and try and loosen up a bit.'

I did as he said.

At last he said, 'Enough,' and looked at me in silence, deep in thought. After a while he gave his judgement.

'You're coming to see me properly next Saturday, aren't you?'

'Yes,' I murmured. The somewhat ignoble thought crossed my mind that he was checking on the forth-coming fee.

'Well, we've a lot to do. Your grip's far too strong, you don't bend your knees enough, you fail to bring your body round enough on the back swing and don't get your weight off your left side, so you suffer from a severe reverse weight transfer. Your weight then falls back on to the right side just when it ought to be moving forward.'

He paused.

'You lose your balance at the top of the swing and overcock your wrists, which you then uncock to give your shot power, the rest of your body being all over the place, particularly your head, which sways too freely.'

He paused.

'Those are the main problems. You've a few other minor difficulties, which we'll need to think about if we're going to get you down to single figures.'

Thoughts of the dentist returned. Three large cavities in A, B and D, the need for a crown on the lower incisor and the removal of all four wisdom teeth – apart from that, they'll be in perfect condition with regular brushing and morning and evening flossing. I felt sick.

'Isn't there anything I can do about tomorrow?' I asked feebly.

He regarded me with pity. I suppose he saw the need to temper justice with mercy.

'For tomorrow, forget everything I've just said. Play your normal game.' The words were obviously difficult to say for he frowned. 'Just remember two things. First, swing slowly, and secondly, try to get your weight on to the front foot when you hit the ball. Put it another way, relax and swing through the ball. Enjoy your golf.'

At that moment the final words of advice seemed preposterous, so I smiled bravely. 'Well, thank you very much, Andy,' I said and shook his hand.

As I was about to leave Andy added, 'The young woman I was coaching before you is looking for a partner for the under-25s mixed foursomes. She's a new member and her name's Celia Brunner. You might want to ask her. She could be good.'

'Oh, thanks,' I answered, somewhat disconcerted. It had not occurred to me before to mix business with pleasure.

The next day's golf was a peculiar affair. I had woken early and lain in bed considering Andy's advice. I was of course aware I suffered from a tendency to reverse pivot, and I allowed my right hand to slip too far under the club to compensate my tendency to block with the wrists, but

I wondered if he really meant I should relax and enjoy it. As I lay there I came to the conclusion that as a piece of advice it was a veiled, or not so veiled, insult. I knew perfectly well what I needed to do to get a little more out of it, not give up the task by swinging with gay abandon.

So as Dai and I stood on the first tee, with a brisk south-wester threatening to take any hook into the windscreens of the oncoming traffic, my head was full of the little checklist that I found so handy. So it appeared was Dai's.

'Did you get your lesson, Jim?'

'Not really, Andy just gave me a few ideas.'

'Hard luck. He managed to give me three-quarters of an hour. Very handy.'

'Oh, I doubt it'll make much difference, judging by the few tips he gave me,' I said ungraciously.

'We'll see.'

'We certainly will. It'll have to have been an excellent lesson to make up for your late night.'

'Did I wake you when I came in?'

'Not at all; I was just judging by the bags under your eyes.'

I suppose you'd say I had a bad attitude, but he did seem awfully smug that morning after some lousy party he'd been to, which he'd been telling us about in advance all week.

He hit his first ball hard and long, holding its course down the middle of the fairway despite the wind. I hit a pretty good one, too, but it had a little draw and ended in the long rye grass in the ditch beside the road.

'You brought your shoulders round and didn't get your hips through,' said Dai helpfully.

'There's a lot of wind up there,' I replied.

I hacked out and crafted a sliced ball to a hundred and fifty yards short of the green. He hit a long three-iron which fell firmly and ran on a little way. He pitched practically dead. I sliced my fourth, failed to sink my fifth from off the green and picked up.

On the next I tried to allow for the slice that seemed to be dominating my game up to that point and hit a perfect seven, straight as a die into the left-hand bunker. He was twenty feet from the hole. I exploded out and putted close. He putted straight but long, missed the return and we halved.

'You're hitting the ball awfully well,' I said after he had put another drive straight down the middle.

'Yes, Andy's a marvel, isn't he?'

'Pity he didn't spend more time on your putting.'

Dai continued to play like a god. Even his putting came right and he walked on to the tee of the tenth as a man who could do no wrong. I, on the other hand, had speeded up my swing, slowed it down, turned my hands round to weaken my grip, reduced my wrist cock so I was hitting the ball like a marshmallow, and even closed my stance to compensate for everything else. It was only because I was chipping and putting with unusual accuracy that I was only four down. It occurred to me later that I had practised neither.

'Gosh, I'm enjoying this. What a great game golf is!'

He stood on the tee two over for the first nine, at least three shots better than he had ever done before.

I can truly say that at that moment I hated him. If ever a man deserved to be struck down by the gods of the golf course, he did. But he wasn't, not exactly, at least.

His next drive went well, very well, but his reading of the line was slightly faulty, and with just the suspicion of a fade it lodged in the long grass on the right-hand corner of the right-handed dog-leg. He found the ball easily enough.

'Not an ideal lie, but I'll go for it.' This was in stark contrast to his normal safety-first approach, but he was playing so well.

'Quite right,' I said, admiration in my voice.

Perhaps he speeded up slightly, perhaps the lie was not like anything on Andy's practice ground, but he thinned it weakly, got caught by some gorse and fell back into an unplayable lie.

'Never mind,' he said in a childlike manner. He dropped his ball for a penalty and put his fourth beside the pin. This really irritated me. I was on the edge in two, left my putt short and we halved.

It was still his honour.

'Into this wind you won't even be able to think about driving the green,' I said.

'No, but I can cut off quite a bit of the lake.'

Perhaps he hurried things a bit, because he didn't cut off any of the lake, the wind again just sliding him over, off his line.

'Hard luck,' I said sportingly. At this stage I regarded his misfortune as nothing more than a respite. It was, in my view, all hopeless, four down, eight to play, and playing like a drain. The lake was obviously going to catch my slice. Who cares – I thought, as I stood there – I might as well just whack it. Whack it I did, and to my amazement, and Dai's, it flew straight and high, leaving me a reasonable approach to the green.

As we walked up the fairway my spirits had revived enough for me to remark, 'You've been having an excellent round, even with your little trouble here.'

'I think my left heel is coming up a bit far on the back swing.'

I made no comment immediately, but thought deeply about my reply. Eventually I managed, 'Yes, but only a fraction.'

The game continued on its way. I can't say I improved much, but at least I started to enjoy it. I'm not quite sure why, really. Certainly it's more fun if the game is close, and it did get closer.

At two down on the sixteenth I saw Dai agonising over his grip as he addressed the ball. He kept opening and closing alternate eyes, concentrating like a hypnotist on his hands. I thought of chiding him to hurry up, but felt it more sporting to contribute to the evident inner debate.

'It's the third knuckle that's the problem, isn't it?'

Naturally I was referring to his left hand. He looked up as though coming out of a daze.

'How did you know?'

'Oh, all the books say so. Not just Andy, you know.'

'I know that, but how did you know it was my particular problem?'

Here I must admit I embroidered things a bit, but I did think it might help.

'Always thought it was, but didn't like to say.'

'Well, you're so right.'

He concentrated again after this repartee and eventually hit it with ferocity. His swing was now quite fast, like a man wishing to get on to the next shot but one, and the result was less than perfect.

Now it was my turn to concentrate. Gone was the carefree rhythm of a few holes earlier. I duly sliced it high on to the bench which overlooks the fifteenth green, leaving me a long way to go up the sixteenth. But if my concentration was giving me problems, Dai was now like a chess grandmaster faced with mate in two. He was swivelling the club around in his hands before each shot, taking endless practice swings, all quite smooth, then hitting the ball with such speed and aggression that he must have been jarring his wrists terribly. He was in such a state that I thought at one point we were going to hold up the people behind, the unforgivable sin at St Wilfrid's.

We were all square to the last. By now we were two punchdrunk boxers, swinging wildly but to little effect. As the great Capablanca once said – I translate freely – remarking on the brilliance of the combat of two lesser chess players, 'They continually defeat me in their ability to find a move worse than the worst I can imagine.' So it was with Dai and me.

I hit the plate-glass window of the clubhouse with my second but it bounded back safely. Dai put his third on to the pump house roof. We eventually scrabbled sixes.

Despite the draw our frames of mind were very different, as we left the eighteenth green on our way for two hardly deserved pints of bitter.

'I'm going to see if I can get a midweek lesson off Andy,' mumbled Dai.

'Never mind, you played some glorious golf. I was lucky to get a half,' I said cheerily. I felt cheery.

'What are you so happy about?' grunted Dai.

'Oh, I don't know,' I replied.

But actually I did. I had decided to ring up Andy the next morning, cancel my golf lesson, offering to pay, of course. Then I would invite Celia Brunner to play with me in the mixed foursomes. It was tips like that which were the real purpose of the golf pro.

As Andy predicted, Miss Brunner proved to be a rather good golfer, but I think I should take most of the credit for that.

Terms of Engagement

(elia turned out to be the perfect golf partner, for mixed foursomes at least. Our first outing was to be the Lady Captain's Meeting, no less. When I arrived at the putting green, my statutory thirty minutes before tee-off time, I was impressed to see her already there, practising her curiously slow putting stroke.

I was even more impressed by her sensible clothes. One of the great virtues of golf is that there is really no dress code, at least not at any decent club. Of course one draws the line at tucked-in trousers, jeans and suchlike, but not in any foolish Jeevesian way, and one does have standards about things like caps, any colour but yellow, but so long as you wear something nondescript, easy on the eye, you can be as shabby as you like.

Well, we know that women have a thing about their clothes, which I think goes back to those taffeta dresses their mothers put them in at their childhood birthday parties. And it takes a woman of real character to kick those early influences, incredible character to resist the temptation when they're on a public arena like a golf course. Well, Celia had resisted the temptation manfully, if you see what I mean.

She was dressed in a pair of darkish tartan plus-fours and a dark blue polo-neck sweater. I only tell you to give you the idea of how thoroughly normal she looked. Her golf shoes were light brown brogues. Jeeves would have purred.

'Hello, Celia, glad to see you're knuckling down.' As the senior member of the team I wanted to show my approval. She smiled – a little nervously, I thought.

We had had a drink the evening before in the King's Head in the old town. I'd thought of giving her dinner, but reflected it would be better to keep our relationship strictly golf. After all, I'd learnt from Sammy that pleasure and golf is a poor cocktail. I had impressed on her, however, as she sipped a bitter lemon, that I regarded the whole event as no more than a pleasant excuse for a walk. All she needed to do was to play her normal game and, as I rather unwisely put it, I'd do the rest.

I realised as we finished our drinks and prepared to depart that there was one thing in particular on her mind. She said rather quietly, 'I've never played with Mrs McVittie. All the girls say she's a stickler for the rules.'

'Oh, don't worry about that,' I'd said encouragingly. 'So am I.'

As it turned out she was a delight to play with, that first day. I talked her round and she responded like a natural. 'Look just push it up the fairway and I'll put us safely on in three.' – 'Anywhere on the green will do.' – 'The rough's a bit deep there, treat it with respect.' – 'We don't need to sink it, just close' – and she played to instructions without demur, often improving on them. It was no surprise we were challenging for the lead at the end of the first round.

Andy, our friendly pro, was there in the ladies' bar for a change, deserting the hard-drinking set in the real bar. He was smiling benignly on his charges, who were frisking round him like sixth-form girls around the English master, belying their fifty years and some.

'Well, you two are there or thereabouts,' he addressed Celia and me with condescension.

'What are we up against?' An obvious enough question.

'Where did you finish?' he countered, but before I could answer we were interrupted by the Lady Vice-Captain with some fatuous question about free-dropping in a hazard, and he turned his attention to more important fish.

I shepherded Celia with her half of lager shandy to a corner of the ladies' bar and we settled down. After a few sips I realised she was sitting very still. I suddenly saw why certain golfers are called rabbits, but she had played well above herself.

'From what I can see we are in the top four or five. Thirty-five stableford points is more than respectable on the course today.'

She raised her lager carefully. 'Thank you,' she said quietly.

'We've quite a bit of homework to do, you know,' I said in a captain's fashion.

'If you say so, Jim, but I thought we did rather well.' I noticed for the first time that she did have an awfully sweet smile.

She seemed, all the same, rather uneasy in the formal surroundings of the great club. 'Why don't we have dinner together in town and we can plan it out?'

'That would be lovely.'

We drove into the ancient town and up to the Royal George near the top of the hill, below the church. I wanted to keep the focus on the golf, and between our avocado, her sole *bonne femme* and my steak Diane, we planned our strategy for the next day.

'Driving the evens as today, there is really one responsibility – put it on the fairway. If you do that we should be able to repeat today's score, and some.'

It was a bold thing to say, and I detected a slight smile of admiration, I think.

'You see,' I continued, 'if you give me a reasonable go with my second there's no reason we shouldn't be challenging par on a number of holes. Admittedly I shall play short on the sixth, but with your short irons we could even pick up a four there.'

She had given up trying to dig the remaining corners out of her avocado, which was perhaps a little on the fresh side, but she clearly did not disagree with the main bones of the strategy.

'On the eighth, so long as I don't carve one into the thorns a par should be no trouble.'

'I wish I had your self-confidence,' she said wistfully. I sympathised.

'Even on the thirteenth we don't need to take any chances. Just put it up to the plateau and I'll turf it over on to the green and we'll be solid for a five.'

Well, we all know about mice and men, but as so often at St Wilfrid's the weather played its cruel part. When you have a cold northwesterly buffeting you, it's not only your ball that gets dragged into unexpected places. It's almost as if some of your brain cells are being downloaded away from the central processing unit and so cannot function in the required manner. Of course it's childish to blame the wind. The fact is that plans are awfully difficult to keep to in the heat of battle.

Nor was it entirely my fault. On the fourth, for example, she put it on the fairway all right, but it was so short, and to the left-hand side to boot, that a three-iron into the wind only had to have the barest fade to roll off down the hill to the right. And then she left me on the top part of the green so I had a delicate downhill putt. Not surprisingly, I put it a little way past. The return should not have been beyond her, even if six feet or so, perhaps more.

In the ladies' bar afterwards she was even more tongue-tied, but I felt there was a need to dissect the round, if only to do justice to the plan of the night before.

'I don't think the plan actually did us any harm,' I said.

She made a sort of umming sound.

'The fourteenth worked like a dream. You short of the green, I chipped dead and you holed it.'

She was about to say something so I corrected myself slightly.

'Well, perhaps it wasn't that dead, but you put it away easily enough.'

Suddenly she became quite animated. 'The three-footer on the third, the long iron on the fourth, the thorns on the eighth, the gorse on the tenth, the swans on the eleventh, the pot bunker on the twelfth, the pump house on the fifteenth, the giant parsley on the sixteenth, the chip and the second bunker shot on the seventeenth, and the clubhouse roof on the last.'

You may have gathered from this that we were not challenging for the silverware on this particularly wet and windy day. But a man has to defend himself.

'Would you like another lager shandy, partner?' I offered.

As I made my way between the broad shoulders of the flower of English womanhood, it did occur to me that Celia had not played without fault. Still, gallantry is my middle name.

'This'll cheer you up,' I said, passing her the half. 'After all, golf was sent to humble us, and you do play off twenty.'

She didn't look at me but mumbled something to the effect that some people don't even notice when they make mistakes. For a silly moment I thought she was talking about me, but I dispelled the idea.

'What we should do is put our names down for the Alexander Cup, you know, the summer bank holiday competition, and come storming back at them.' I thought this would show her that I really had confidence in her.

I was a little surprised by the *froideur* in her reply, 'Let me think about it,' and on the way back in the car she gave me her decision. 'I think you'd better find someone else for the Alexander Cup.'

I was stunned. Not play with me in the top summer mixed competition! The woman was out of her mind. There were half a dozen women who would have given their all, and more, to partner me – perhaps I exaggerate – and this slip of a girl dared to suggest . . .Well, it was absurd. Desperate situations call for desperate actions.

'How about dinner and a film on Wednesday evening?' It was indeed a desperate throw, particularly as Wednesday was my snooker night, but I knew it was her rule not to go out more than once during the week.

'I'll think about it,' she said.

'Come on, Celia, we make a great team.'

'Do you really think so?'

'Of course I do. We're made for each other.'

'You didn't seem to think so on the course today.'

'Nonsense. You were great. It was my fault we didn't do better.' Sometimes you have to bend the truth in the interests of compromise.

She put her hand on mine as I changed gear and gave me a little kiss behind the ear. 'You are a funny old thing.'

I took this in the spirit in which I believed it was intended and, as we pulled up outside her flat, I confirmed the situation. 'So I'll put us down for the Alexander Cup.'

'We can talk about it on Wednesday.' I must say I had rather assumed Wednesday had been deferred in the light of our rapprochement, and I was even more shocked when she added, 'And by the way, I did tell Johnny Douglas that I might partner him if today didn't go well.'

I sat in gloom as she tripped off to her cosy home. The humiliation of losing Celia as a partner was a threat of gargantuan proportions.

I tossed and turned that night, and lived through that Wednesday evening in prospect in a variety of half-waking dreams. In all of them Johnny Douglas floated like an evil presence.

As it happened Wednesday evening went well, very well in fact. Celia had decided to get out a video of that Bond movie, *Goldfinger*, exciting stuff, only spoiled by the unrealistic golf game.

She cooked a first-rate dinner, steak *au poivre* with a bottle of claret, mangetout and so forth. Over dinner we skirted round the subject between us, until at last I brought it to a head.

'The thing is, I think you are the one for me.'

'Oh, Jim, do you mean it?'

'I've thought about it, and yes, I do.'

'I can hardly believe it. I thought you had gone off me after last weekend.'

'Off you! Don't be ridiculous, Celia. All I've thought about is you.'

'Oh, Jim, it's so wonderful to hear you say it.'

You can imagine my joy, tinged with relief. My partnership problems were over. It was only over coffee that some slight confusion arose.

Interlocking her fingers with mine across the table, not just overlapping, she said, 'I suppose we should think about dates.'

'Oh, don't worry about that. It's the Monday of the summer bank holiday.'

'You are a silly chap. I don't mean the golf, I mean us.'

'Oh, us,' I said, perhaps a little vaguely. Then the penny dropped. *Us?* My head span, probably my eyes rolled and my knees turned to jelly. Had I grounded my club in a hazard inadvertently?

Us? I thought. But why not? Think of a ready-made golf partner for golf holidays in Portugal!

I was perhaps a little silent, and there was a funny tone to Celia's voice as she followed up with, 'Jim, you do mean it, don't you? You were talking about us, weren't you?'

I was resolved. 'Of course, Celia, of course,' and we interlocked our fingers.

So is the course of our lives determined and, looking back, I have no regrets, taking the rough with the smooth, the long with the short.

The honeymoon was a bit of a surprise, however. I had booked a holiday on the Algarve. It looked over the rolling Atlantic on one side and a great swathe of the fourth fairway of a fine golf course on the other.

I must say I think the comings and goings of two people on their honeymoon should be kept pretty private, but I'll give you a flavour of what happened.

We woke on the first morning of our married life after an excellent dinner of avocado salad and lobster. I was full of beans and couldn't wait for our tee-off time at nine.

'Sorry, darling Jim,' issued this disembodied voice from the bedclothes, 'but I've got an awful headache.'

It was a blow but I found the pro and had a most enjoyable eighteen with him. Celia was beside the pool when I got back.

'I'm feeling much better, thank you, dear.'

The day went well and so did the evening, but I have to say that the next morning was again a let-down. 'I don't know what the matter is with me, Jim, but I've got this awful pain,' she said, rubbing her forehead.

The pattern was set and, although we had a wonderful honeymoon in almost every respect, Celia's headaches came between her and the course. It was on the plane home that I confronted the problem.

'I think we should face up to this like two mature human beings.'

'Yes,' said Celia in a small voice.

'Whatever we expected from each other when we got married, if at the end of the day you don't want to play the game, I can't force you.'

'Oh, Jim, do you mean it?'

It was a blow, a terrible blow, but I took it like a man.

'Yes, Celia, I do.'

Well, there you are. It was probably for the best, after all. Golf is a very private thing and if it doesn't work you can't force it.

The Noble Art of Finding Golf Balls

I'm not sure you're actually any better than me.'

It was a rather petulant remark from my dear cousin. He played golf only a few times a year, during his holiday in the Algarve and at St Wilfrid's during his annual week-end with me and mine.

He had a notional handicap of 22, and I was a well-practised 15. I gave him the full difference and beat him, two and one or thereabouts.

'The difference between us is not golf at all, it's just that you're better at finding the ball than I am.'

The sun was sliding down behind St Wilfrid's Harbour and to the shine of the coarse grass of the rough was added deep long shadows. When we had come up the eighteenth half an hour ago, it had already been a test of a well-trained sniffer dog. By now any ball off the fairway would be an impossible challenge.

'Don't be silly, Freddy. The idea of golf is to go from tee to fairway to green. You go into the rough and you lose your ball. That's why you're worse than me. You can't hit the ball straight.'

'You were in the rough just as much as me. You just happen to be better at finding balls.'

'Nonsense! Listen, Freddy, you forget I play golf every

weekend. I'm bound to be better than you. I hit the ball better, straighter.'

'But you don't. Take the first hole. You hooked the ball into that lush stuff just short of the dip, and you went straight to it.'

'Of course. That's where I hit it last weekend.'

'Exactly. And on the third you were up on the bank going up to the fourth fairway, as was I. You found your ball. I didn't find mine.'

'No, I did.'

'That's my point. You're very good at finding golf balls. In fact I counted. On the first nine, I was in the rough seven times. You found my ball five times. I found it once. Once it was lost, on the seventh.' He took a large gulp from his vodka and tonic. 'On the second nine it was a different story. I was in the rough five times. I found it once. You found it once. And I lost three. Whether you were looking quite so hard for my ball on the second nine—'

'Are you suggesting . . .?!' I interrupted. It was typical Freddy and I was not amused.

'No, of course not, though perhaps subconsciously—'

'That's unworthy of you!'

'No, no, I don't mean that. All I mean is, you are better at finding your ball. And that is the decisive difference.'

It was really preposterous. Freddy has always been the intellectual of the family. Looks it too, bald with a polished dome. Not a donnish intellectual, I will give him, but too clever by half really, even though he's had quite a successful time in the City of London. So we've all got used to his theorising. Still, he does tend to go too far.

'Listen, Freddy, why don't you take up golf seriously and try to beat me with no excuses?'

'I've got a better idea. I'm going back tomorrow evening, but let's have one more game. This time we'll level things up and have a test of golf, not hunt the thimble.' He had another swig of his Vod. and T. 'We'll each have a caddy. When the ball goes into the rough only our caddies are allowed to find the ball.'

'One caddy per ball or two caddies for both balls?'

'Two caddies for both balls. That makes it fair.'

'It's absurd.' The whole thing was getting out of hand. As a married man, I had grown used to taking it easy on Sunday mornings. I had an understanding better half, but to play the next day, on a Sunday, would have been more than my life was worth.

'If we start at 8 AM sharp we'll be round by 11:15 at the latest, and we can have pre-lunch drinks with your lady wife.'

'For goodness' sake, Freddy, why don't you take up golf seriously instead of all this theorising? Anyway, we won't get caddies at that time.'

Freddy looked momentarily dismayed at the thought of it being too early for caddies, but he was nothing if not energetic. He jumped up, polished off his poison and left the bar.

I cursed my luck. The whole thing was futile. He was bound to lose. It was just a waste of time, to be balanced against my duties as a host.

He returned in five minutes full of bounce, like a golf ball on the road at the twelfth. 'No problem, no problem at all. At first your pro was a bit frosty, but I explained the whole thing and he said it would be fine. Two caddies at 7:45 sharp.'

'What about Celia?'

'No problem there, either. I spoke to her. She's quite happy.'

It was true, up to a point. Celia took it well. I think she rather relished being able to get up on a Sunday morning in her own time, and not having to make me breakfast. It seemed a dangerous precedent. She also seemed to be highly amused at how angry I was at the whole thing, a joke she shared with Freddy. The situation was made worse by Freddy drinking rather a lot of our local's red plonk, while I had to go easy.

'Really, dear, you seem to be rather off your juice.'

'Staying sober for tomorrow, old chap?' chimed in Freddy.

'Well, you want to play at this ungodly hour. I don't want it made worse by a hangover.'

'Very wise, old chap. Pass the bottle, Celia.' And he took yet another glass. 'As far as I'm concerned an early morning game is just the ticket, especially at your venerable club.'

Then he frowned and became even more animated, in his pompous way. 'Your club, your club, it isn't really your club at all. You just happen to be a member. Passing through, as it were. Who owns the club?'

'The members, of course!' I interrupted his soliloquy.

'They think they do, and in law no doubt they do, but they can't transfer their ownership, they can't sell it; when they die their heirs don't inherit it. Not much of an ownership.' He stopped to polish off another glass and refilled it. That at least was another nail in his coffin for the following day.

'Steady on, Freddy, I don't want to win on a technical knockout.'

'I've never found a slight muzziness from the night before a problem. Helps me to keep my head steady, though not still of course. And I keep my whole game at about eighty-five per cent power. Perfect. Nothing as dangerous as a wounded golfer, old chap.'

'We'll see.'

'But where was I, Celia? Oh yes, ownership. The game is all about ownership, you know. The club is only the superficial part. The real question of ownership turns on the ball. It's a game about possession and making your mark. Not just chasing a little white ball, it's chasing *your* little white ball. The ball you took out of your bag at the first tee, sent hurtling off into space, recovered from the middle of the fairway two hundred and fifty yards away, stroked up to the pin and holed for a birdie.'

'You wish,' I growled.

'Don't be unkind, dear,' said Celia.

'It's quite understandable, Celia. He's jealous of my deeper appreciation of the game of golf. Though he is of course a fine player, even a better one, as may or may not be proved tomorrow.'

'Thank you, cousin.'

'But you are obsessional. You have to be. And that's why you find your ball. You have the necessarily obsessional interest in possession. I, as you know, am not blessed with it.'

'And I suppose because you're not obsessional you lose.'

'Not tomorrow, Josephine! You'll see.'

'There, there, boys,' said Celia with a laugh.

When I saw our caddies through the sea mist at 7:45 in the morning I realised that what had begun as a bad idea and deteriorated now promised to be a source of lasting misery. They loomed out of the mist in their matching blue anoraks and waterproof trousers. A pang of jealousy, as I realised they were more sensibly clothed than I was, added to my other bitter emotions.

Up to that point I had at least presumed there was no danger of me losing. Now I was not so sure. How Freddy had persuaded our good-natured pro to supply old Dick Dunstable and his grandson Rick, I don't know, but it was the final straw.

I couldn't contain myself. 'What on earth are you doing here, Dick?'

It was not polite but it was an honest reaction.

'Well, Andy said Mr South was looking for a caddy and would I help out and, seeing as how you had given us such a good day not so long ago, I said, "Why not?"'

I tried to keep the sarcasm out of my voice. 'Most generous of you, I'm sure, Dick. And at this time of day.'

'Well, I don't sleep as I used to and it does young Rick good to get up before noon once in a while, doesn't it, Rick?'

Rick grunted, removed his steel-rimmed glasses, and tried to polish them in the gloaming.

So this was our friendly pro's idea of a joke. I could well imagine how he had sold it: 'You know Jim South, who you played with on Caddies' Day? Well, he and his cousin have a big money game and need a couple of caddies. It would give you a chance to enjoy yourself and earn a few quid.'

'What, that geezer who couldn't sink a six-incher and kept asking me to stop moving about while he played? Oh, it will be a pleasure to caddy for him! And Rick's got his usual bad head cold, so I'll bring him if you need a pair.'

Of course I'm making this dialogue up. Old Dick would have been more measured in his response, but it would have meant exactly the same.

Well, so there was old Dick thumping his fist into his hand and young Rick polishing his glass orbs, and Freddy looking as fresh as a daisy, and I was feeling like death not very warmed up.

'Good morning, gents,' said Freddy. 'Delighted you're both here. Let me explain the rules. Mr South and I have agreed not to look for any balls in the rough. That's up to you. Otherwise, normal caddying. Oh, and I agreed with Andy, I'll pay double normal rates.'

Then, turning to me, he added so that the two Dunstables could hear, 'Obviously, Jim, since this is my experiment I'll pay for them both.'

'Do stop talking about the caddies as if they didn't exist,' I whispered to Freddy. 'Dick Dunstable is a distinguished member of the Caddies' Association.'

'Quite, quite,' murmured Freddy, obviously delighted at my discomfiture. 'Even so, someone has to pay them, and I'm offering.'

I saw no point in not recouping some of my expense, so I demurred briefly and without enthusiasm.

Freddy's game was exactly as per normal. He missed the fairway regularly on both sides. His ball was found most of the time. In fact, by the time we got to the eighteenth he had lost only one.

It was my game that suffered. What with Dick going, 'Tch, tch,' when I missed a three-footer on the fourth, a horrible sloping fast green, and his awful grandson removing his misted glasses on my back-swing between sniffs, my game lost most of its rhythm.

I should also say that there's nothing more frustrating than standing in the middle of the fairway while two caddies, one old, the other blind, and both indolent, wander around looking for your ball when you know exactly where it is.

After a while I formed the view that they actually identified both our balls more or less at once and then spent the rest of the five minutes seeing if they could find a few strays, which they quickly pocketed. By the fifteenth their pockets were full.

Anyway, by the time we got to the eighteenth we were still all square. It was only all square and not all over because the two, Dick and Rick, had failed to find my tee shot on the seventeenth. I had hit a fine three-iron, but its draw had been taken by the wind and what should have been on the edge of the green was well into the rough stuff.

'That'll take a bit of finding,' said Freddy in a sepulchral tone, and I suspected he winked at old Dick. My suspicions grew fiercer when, about halfway through the search, Dick stopped as though he had found a ball, but then stumbled on and did not return to the spot.

'So, all square to the last. A fitting climax.' Freddy was purring with confidence.

'Watch out for those bushes on the right,' I said unsportingly.

'Don't worry, the boys are ready for me.' They were indeed stationed in the best place for his slice.

The pleasure of golf is the predictability of your opponent's bad shot. I knew with absolute certainty that Freddy's determination to slice would bring on a hook. It did. Off it went, not a duck hook but a hard low racing ball, clearing the hillocks about 120 yards forward and careering down into the ravine, embedding itself in the bank. Of course we couldn't see it from the tee, but I knew the thick grass there and I felt that special elation of the golf opponent, almost superior to one's admiration of one's own brilliance.

I stood up to the tee and hit a good high ball. It had mild fade, but I reckoned it would have kept out of the thorns and probably be on the edge of the fairway, more or less where the two caddies waited. The hole looked as good as mine, and the match.

It was pretty irritating to find Dick standing over a spot in the long grass above Freddy's ball. It was even more irritating to find young Rick ambling about on the edge of the fairway with no sign of my ball.

The seconds were turning into minutes and there was still no sign. Freddy's smirk was broadening and I was fulminating. 'For goodness' sake, Rick, you were standing there, you must have seen it land.'

'Sorry, Mr South, but I didn't. It came so quick.'

'Of course it did, that's what balls do.'

'The boy's trying his hardest, sir, we're both trying our

hardest. You should've put it on the fairway,' chipped in old Dick.

'He should've cleaned his glasses.'

'You can't blame him for that, Mr South, he keeps them clean all right.'

'Well I do blame him.'

'It's all that reading he does,' and then filling with grandpaternal pride, added, 'he's going to university at Oxford next year you know, Mr South.'

'Good show,' I countered without a pause. 'Maybe he could find my golf ball in the meantime.'

Perhaps I was a little harsh on the boy, but there were far too many intellectuals on the course at St Wilfrid's that particular morning.

Then I saw the ball. It was three feet off the fairway in some slightly longer grass.

'There it is.' The words were out of my mouth before I realised their significance.

'So it is, old chap. But you've lost. You've found your own ball.'

'No, I haven't, it's on the fairway.'

'Don't be ridiculous, it's in the long grass.'

'Yes, but that's just a ridge of grass. The fairway doesn't end there.'

'Of course it does.'

'Anyway, I can play the ball without leaving what is obviously fairway. So, even if the ball is in the rough, I'm on the fairway. And the rule was, we weren't allowed to leave the fairway until the ball was found. Well, I haven't. And I'll hit the ball without leaving the fairway.'

'Okay, Jim.' Freddy had looked at the position and could see that I would have more than a little difficulty stretching over to play the ball. 'Okay, Jim, why not bend the rules? It's only a game.'

You'd be surprised how difficult it is to hit a ball which is six inches further away from where you normally hit it. And I needed to take a three-iron to reach anywhere near the green, when the lie demanded a six. But I was still in it.

Freddy hacked his ball about seventy yards on to the fairway. I weighed up the options. My extra distance from the ball suggested I would take it on the toe. This would either impart hook, or if I caught it with an open face it would be pushed out weakly into the thicker rough on the bank which fell away to the right. I should tell you that a full-blooded hook would take out the clubhouse picture window at best. At worst, it would disappear into the car park.

I elected to rely on my natural weakness, a slice, and aiming well to the left of the clubhouse I hit a low raking slice with an open face which went about 150 yards, still thirty yards short.

The cousin proceeded to defy all the logic of this infuriating game. Just when the pressure should have made his shot unplayable, he smashed a perfect five-iron to within fifteen feet of the pin.

I rolled up a reasonable chip, but I left it twenty feet short. My putt was not difficult, for a twenty-footer that is, but it just passed the hole to the left.

'Well, this is it, Freddy, just roll it in.' I had taken the flag and was tending it.

'I'll take the flag, sir.' Old Dick ambled up.

'Don't worry, Dick. You take it easy.' My look was not friendly.

I'm glad to say that Freddy was concentrating rather hard on the putt and so did not decide the argument. Old Dick ambled off again.

So there I stood, radiating a psychic barrier around the hole, determined to hold the ball at bay. No doubt Freddy was using equal and opposite psychic force.

He hit the ball calmly and it sped firmly towards the hole with an excellent roll, achieved with a modicum of top spin. My psychic barrier proved sadly ineffectual and the ball dropped into the centre of the cup.

Freddy threw his arms up, his face wreathed in smiles. Old Dick smirked and Rick continued to polish his glasses. I felt sick.

'Well played,' I choked out, but the sight of Freddy walking towards me with his hand outstretched proved too much. I couldn't bring myself to shake it, so I bent down and picked up his ball instead. I'm glad I did.

'What were you playing with, Freddy?'

What were you playing with, Fred, Jim, Tom, Bill, Alex? It doesn't matter who. Glorious words to utter.

Miserable words to hear. Freddy knew exactly what I meant and he froze, like Lot's wife or some poor soul having spied the Gorgon. He rallied.

'What the hell do you mean? You know damn well it's my ball.'

''Fraid not, old sport. It's a Maxfli and you were playing with a Pinnacle.'

'I don't believe it. Here, let me see.'

I walked towards him with the celestial word Maxfli facing him. He took one look at the ball and then wheeled on old Dick. The caddy was picking at some string on the side of the bag, some old green fee ticket I suppose.

'Well, Dick?' asked my cousin in his iciest tone.

'Well, sir?' replied Dick Dunstable at his most innocent. Had I misjudged Dick? Could he really have 'found' the wrong ball, not Freddy's ball, on purpose? I put the thought from my mind. I couldn't face being indebted to Old Dick.

Silence persisted for a moment or two before Freddy spoke again.

'Well played, old chap. Member's privilege, I suppose,' he said, shooting another look at Dick. Then he added halfheartedly, 'Of course, we must try again some other time. After all, the result hardly proves either of us right.'

'Oh, I don't know about that,' I said rather smugly to Freddy's retreating back.

So my happiness was unconstrained, a perfect ending only alloyed by one detail. As I followed, Old Dick sidled up and in a matter-of-fact way said, 'Well, Jim, it's a fine thing to see a member win a hard game like that one.'

The game over he felt entitled to revert to the use of my first name.

'Oh, thank you, Dick,' I replied cautiously.

'You were the better man on the day,' he paused. 'If not at golf, at least at having your ball found.'

He and young Rick laughed together, and the intellectual grandson winked at me through his re-misted glasses. I winked back for some reason. I suppose it was a victory wink.

A Golfing Holiday

'If only we played every day instead of once a week,' lamented Alfred Dickins, the distinguished accountant, as we sat round the statutory pint of golden brew before lunch on Sunday. 'You'd never have missed the green on the last if you weren't just a Sunday golfer.'

In point of fact the wind had been blowing rather hard from the east and it was swirling round the clubhouse before beating down on the eighteenth, so I'm not sure he was right, though I was prepared to agree, since the wind had caught my fade and faded it away into the vicious long stuff beyond the hut.

Bob thought deeply, then, tapping his pipe out in the club ashtray, offered, 'You must be right, Alfred. Or otherwise the pros would only play on Sundays.'

'There's nothing to stop you practising during the week, you know, especially as the evenings draw out,' chipped in Harry with his lopsided smile. It was the only sense in which he ever did chip in, but none the more welcome for that.

'Don't be ridiculous,' Alfred replied haughtily. 'After a day at Clutterbuck's, and supper with the better half in prospect, do you really think I want to destroy my morale with a few hacks on the practice ground?'

We nodded our assent.

'What are you driving at?' asked Bob, sucking portentously on his now empty bowl.

Alfred looked momentarily embarrassed and then, smiling, said, 'Well, I was looking in one of those golf mags the other day and I saw they were advertising cut price deals for golf holidays over the Easter break, or anyway the run-up to Easter.'

I had no notion that a 'golfing holiday' is at best an oxymoron, at worst, well . . .

I blurted out: 'Somewhere nice, I hope?'

'Ireland, actually. The west coast.' It wasn't exactly the Caribbean, but the idea had some appeal.

'Dear old Ireland,' said Bob. 'You can't beat it.'

'We'd better join it,' said Harry, his mouth twisted in mirth. For once Alfred didn't slap Harry down, but smiled weakly.

'I've always wanted to play the west coast. I've only played Dublin,' I volunteered.

'I suppose you lost,' said Harry.

'Shut up,' said Alfred.

'How many days do we get? And, more to the point, what's the damage?' asked Bob, no doubt measuring out the cost in pipe tobacco.

'Well, it's a pretty good deal. We play the great courses of the west, a different one each day, from Saturday to Thursday inclusive, twice a day if we want. We stay at a first-rate hotel and have a car to take us out to each course, and breakfast and supper laid on. The total cost is very reasonable.'

'What do you call reasonable? Are you describing the lie you gave me on the thirteenth?'

'Reasonable, Harry, is reasonable, if you know the meaning of the word.'

'So?' asked Bob.

Alfred took a draw from his golden pint and delivered himself slowly as of weighty words, 'Four hundred and ten pounds, including everything.'

'Everything?' asked Harry.

'Everything,' said Alfred. 'Hotel, food, air tickets, everything.'

'Including booze?' asked Harry.

'Don't be ridiculous.'

'Everything else?' asked Harry, winking.

'It's a Catholic country,' said Bob.

'Does it include VAT?' I asked innocently. I caught Alfred off-guard with this one and he muttered something to the effect that he was sure it did.

'I think you ought to confirm that,' I said. The other two nodded and obviously appreciated my intervention.

'Well, that's settled, then,' said Alfred. 'Subject to VAT, of course,' he added, looking at me in a patronising way.

We looked out over the shiny links, the wind holding the coarse grass flat to the ground, and I think there was at that moment a general sense of tedium, even with those great links of St Wilfrid's which we loved so much.

'It'll be fun to get to see some other courses,' Bob said, speaking for all of us, although no one voiced a creeping sense of disloyalty to our own great club.

'And hone our game to perfection,' said Alfred.

'The grass is always greener,' said Harry.

'It could hardly fail to be after the winter we've had,' I added, rather wittily.

Saturday morning saw us gathering at Gatwick en route for Shannon. Alfred was particularly bossy. He had paid for the tickets and now hung on to them like a boy with a new set of football cards. We had sent him our cheques, or at least Bob and I had; Harry had promised to present his at the airport.

'Here you are, then, now give me my ticket.'

'Certainly not, Harry. I'm the organiser. I'm not having you going off and getting lost.'

'Well, I'm not giving you the cheque.'

'Yes you bloody well are.' Alfred was really getting going.

'There, there, children,' said Bob. 'Give him the cheque and humour the poor man. He thinks he's Livingstone taking us up the Limpopo.'

This resolved the conflict and Harry passed over the cheque with a rather graceless, 'It shouldn't bounce.'

Alfred clenched his teeth and muttered, 'It bloody well better hadn't.'

A Golfing Holiday

The flight was Aer Lingus's best, the air hostesses with those bright Irish faces and the passengers the usual scurvy crew of English holiday-makers which marks the Gatwick off-take, boisterous, good-natured and prepared to return any compliments with interest. The returning folk of the west of Ireland stood out in their ties and jackets and look of prosperity. The people of the two islands off the north-west European land mass mixed in friendly fashion as per normal, when left to themselves of course.

'Great people, the Irish,' said Bob as we piled into the hired Nissan at Shannon airport. 'The chap I was sitting next to gave me a running commentary on the woes of the Irish hotel industry. It was an absolute scream. Every sentence ended with – *and it's all the fault of* Bord Fáilte!' This last was delivered in an execrable Irish accent.

'Careful what you say,' said Harry.

'What do you mean?' Bob bristled.

'I'm part Irish,' said Harry.

'Well, I was being complimentary.'

'That's what you think.'

'Anyway, I'm part Irish too,' said Bob.

'Yes, but you're also part English,' said Harry.

'So are you,' said Bob.

'That's got nothing to do with it,' concluded Harry, as Alfred took the corner rather fast and almost reduced the local populace by half a dozen.

'We really are in Ireland,' I said, laughing. The others didn't join in. I don't really blame them. I've often noticed, flying makes people testy.

Good humour had returned by dinner that evening. The hotel was indeed first class, the rooms were clean and warm and the ambience was A1. We had time for a few holes on the hotel nine-holer, and we all played well above ourselves. I holed a ten-footer to win the decisive skin. Our anticipation of the golf ahead made our nerves tingle – or mine did, anyway.

'Well, we've got five days' golf, counting Thursday morning,' said Alfred, the accountant. 'I suggest we plan it out so that we play every combination of four balls, singles, foursomes, greensomes and so on.'

'I suggest we enjoy ourselves,' said Harry.

'Come on, Harry,' I ventured, 'get into the spirit of it.' The truth was, we were all painfully interested in our own game.

'Let's decide each evening an order of play for the following day,' suggested Bob, and to this compromise Harry assented.

We repaired to bed in good heart, only slightly marred by my happening to look in on Alfred's room.

'That's rather palatial, old chap. Did you pay a supplement?'

'Yes, it's not bad, is it? I think they ran out of singles.'

'Bully for you, you ought to give a party.' But I was a bit peaked, really.

114

Next morning the maître d' inquired greasily of Alfred, 'And did Mr Dickins sleep well?'

I was quick to add, 'And in the honeymoon suite, no less?'

The others joined in, and Alfred looked quite uncomfortable. The price of glory, no doubt.

The first day's golf didn't really count. The course, Ballymullee, was a beautiful old track above the cliffs of the Atlantic, and as I stood on the first tee my breath was literally taken away by a gust from the southwester. For once the extra pint of Guinness, topped off by a Paddy, a coarser Irish whiskey, didn't really steady my head, which was being blown mercilessly off my shoulders. With five days to go I've got to say I had a pure carefree swing on that first tee, and got a really excellent connection.

'Hard luck,' said Alfred without much emphasis, as the ball drove into the teeth of the gale, rose like a seagull and disappeared off to the right over some thick pines.

'High, wide and handsome!' cried Harry.

'Hit another,' said Bob. At least the wind had put out his pipe.

The feeling of exhilaration was only slightly dampened when I repeated the exercise. My fifth, a low racing cut, made the fairway.

When Alfred, who I was playing a singles match with, had followed me with a couple of duck hooks, he said firmly, 'Home of the Mulligan, old boy. We're both on the fairway for one.' I can't say I'm a great lover of the Mulligan in normal circs. It was named after the man himself, who on account of drink used to have back his first drive after lunch. But we *were* in Ireland.

'Agreed,' I said. 'Good old Mulligan.'

'One of the best,' said Harry.

I've got to admit that even with Mulligan's help we both had difficulty breaking ninety, and as we sat down to lunch we found Bob and Harry had had a similar morning.

'Not that it matters,' I said. 'We've four days to go.'

The next day was more like it. Ireland, that is. A soft rain was coming up off the coast, the wind had died and it was perfect scoring weather. We had agreed the night before to play stroke play and really concentrate.

'No Paddy for me,' I said as we settled into the lounge after dinner.

'Jameson is a smoother drink, sir,' said the barman.

'Oh, very well, then.' He served me a double, which slipped down nicely, though without the fire of a Paddy.

Our course on the Monday was another great course, the Dingles. We were playing a four-ball and Harry was my partner. I've got to say that his wisecracks were pretty painful on the first nine, particularly since he seemed intent on hitting through his hangover, not the sort of thing you should inflict on a partner unless you could handle it. Mine, I can honestly say, was well under control.

Fortunately his game and his jokes improved simultaneously and we combined well, since for some reason, just as my game was fitting into place, like a glorious three wood to the green on the eighth with the cliffs waiting disappointed for my slice, I hit a couple of fat ones and chipped carelessly at the seventeenth.

We played a lighthearted foursomes in the afternoon, which Harry and I lost. As we'd won in the morning it didn't amount to much, but I must say Bob and Alfred seemed to attach an awful lot of importance to it.

Dinner was another mellow affair, and we had a rather long session in the bar afterwards. Bob, whom I was partnering the next day, was a bit of a killjoy, but the rest of us got stuck in and chatted of this and that to the wee-wee hours, as the blues has it. My hands were a bit sore, and so were my feet, but my three wood on the eighth, and my four-iron on the fourteenth for that matter, had made me confident that the third day would see my game slip into its ultimate groove.

Tuesday broke clear and bright with about a force four; twenty knots wind-speed to you landlubbers. I must admit I'd have preferred something a little more toned down, greys and beiges perhaps, but one can't complain about the sun in Ireland. I thought of wearing shades but I don't believe you can judge distances as well with Polaroids; they flatten things.

The round at the Old of Kerryside, a new great course, was pleasant enough in its way, but it was spoiled by one thing.

'Don't you think you might contribute to one hole?' said Bob. He was really getting up my nose which, linked to the sun in my eyes, the sand in my mouth and the buzz in my ears, I could have done without.

'If you weren't playing like a boring old man, I might just do that.'

'You're supposed to put it on the fairway, straight, and play for safety to a well-protected green, you jerk.'

'It's no good abusing your partner,' I rejoined.

'Well, you've abused yourself.'

'What are you talking about?' I snarled. Men with pickaxes had started up behind my eyes.

'In the bar last night,' Bob replied in an unpleasant, deliberate way.

'I don't know what you mean.'

Harry smirked. 'Well, that's all right, then.'

'Don't join in,' joined in Alfred.

'This was meant to be a holiday.' It may have sounded rather feeble, but I find nothing more irritating than people who can't let themselves go once in a while.

Dinner that evening was subdued. Bob had repaired to bed early with a head cold and Harry had said he rather fancied checking out the action in town, Kinsale, a fifteen-mile drive away.

A Golfing Holiday

The conversation was desultory as Alfred tried to work out the results of all the matches to date. The trouble was that the ground rules were unclear.

'I make it I've won two, lost one and drawn one,' I said.

'You're forgetting you lost the foursome on Tuesday afternoon.'

'That was a friendly. It didn't count.'

'Don't be ridiculous, Jim, we thrashed you.'

'I suppose you're counting the five holes on Saturday evening?'

'No, but everything else was golf. We played for golf balls, so it must have counted.'

You see how petty people can become? I'm glad to say I'm above it, so I changed the subject.

'I hope there's a decent main course this evening. I'm fed up with stew masquerading as casserole.'

'And you're forgetting your stroke-play card had two strokes added for grounding your club in the water hazard.'

'Do grow up, Alfred.'

Over the coffee Alfred mused, 'Well, only two days to go. I suppose our golf will suddenly perk up, after all this play.'

'It's about as likely as Harry getting lucky in Kinsale,' I responded.

'Strange things happen.'

My next remark I'm not particularly proud of. 'I suppose Harry's children are living evidence.'

Alfred studied his coffee in noncommittal fashion.

★

We were on the first tee as arranged at 9:30. The anticipation of that first day had gone. My back ached, my hands were sore so that I had to hold the club lightly and my middle toe was bruised, but my head was clear. Walking wounded, maybe, but still walking. Any physical miseries I felt were, however, fully dispelled by the sight that came to the tee. It hobbled, it grimaced and most wonderfully it sported a real shiner, already richly purple and indigo, glowing like a planetary black hole.

'What on earth happened to you?' inquired Alfred frostily.

'Nothing, really.'

'I hope the car's all right.'

'The car's fine.'

'Well, that's all right, then,' said Bob.

'Got lucky, eh?' I volunteered perhaps a little maliciously, and I won't repeat the exact words Harry used in reply, but they would have been somewhat more common on board ship.

Wednesday turned out to be my day; for golf, that is. The annoying thing was that the lecherous old cripple with his half-closed left eye proved to be almost unstoppable. Gripping the club lightly, and walking slowly, I hardly put a foot wrong, but Harry also found his disabilities a great advantage and since his were, it has to be admitted, larger than mine, he and Bob proved victorious by one hole. You will not be surprised perhaps that the improvement in my game did not compensate for defeat.

'I think I'll take the afternoon off,' I said over lunch in a matter-of-fact way.

'You can't,' said Alfred.

'I bloody well can,' said I.

'Well, you'll forfeit your match. Bob'll have a walkover.'

'I would anyway,' said Bob.

'There's racing at the Curragh this afternoon and I'm going to sit in front of the box and enjoy it in style.'

'Sounds good,' said Harry.

Well, Alfred continued with his scoring in a friendly played with Bob, the result of which I don't have the faintest idea, and Harry and I lost a few tens of Irish pounds.

The last morning we can draw a veil over. Alfred was so far ahead that he had won the three bottles of whiskey, whatever the outcome, and the course, apart from being great, was also long and tight. The sun shone beautifully, a light breeze blew and the clouds were in their appointed place, magnificent towers of cotton wool, not the slabs of slate we had expected, nor the enveloping fog of golfing war. But that shining orb mocked our efforts at golf on that final day. We made the shade of the clubhouse, hot and exhausted from the accumulation of five days' swinging a piece of misshapen metal, Alfred and I especially shattered having lost five and four. Frankly I couldn't hit a thing, and couldn't care less at that.

Only at the airport did my good humour partially return.

'Well, I'm very glad to have seen the south-west. I might bring Celia down for a holiday.'

'Given up the unequal struggle? Goodbye to the old mashie-niblick? Adieu to the hallowed fairway and the welcoming green?' asked Harry.

For an extraordinary moment the vista opened up. Walking round gardens and parks without imagining what it would be like to pitch over the ornamental lake on to the small patch of grass beside the distant rockery, no more swaying of the hips with bent shoulders and rear sticking out while I waited in the queue at the super-market, no more of that sickening flutter in the stomach in the car park before the monthly medal, no more . . . But what was the use?

'Don't be daft, Harry.' I hesitated. 'But the holiday has shown me that there are one or two things in golf apart from life.'

'You mean the other way round,' said Bob.

'Yes, of course I do, other things apart from golf.'

'Such as Jameson and Paddy,' said Bob.

'Or, in Harry's case, black eyes.'

We were waiting in the bar for a while; the plane had been delayed a few minutes. Alfred said, 'I'll just pop off to the gents. Look after my bags, will you?'

'Of course,' said Harry, with a sudden glint in his eye, and he was on his feet as soon as Alfred had disappeared round the corner. It was the work of a moment for him to scrabble in Alfred's bag and produce the tickets.

'Steady on, old chap. That is Alfred's bag, you know,' I said, perhaps a little pompously.

'Of course it is, you creep.' He was studying the tickets with the intensity usually reserved for marking his stableford card. At last he cried out, 'Ah ha! Just as I thought.' He slapped the fan of tickets in his hand with venom. 'Seventy-five pounds return for you, Bob, seventy-five return for you, Jim, seventy-five for me, and' – waving the tickets vigorously – 'zero pounds, zero pence for Alfred Dickins . . . And he got the suite at the hotel,' he added, growling like an angry cur.

'Well, I do think that's a pretty poor show,' I said.

'Poor show? Poor show? Bloody criminal, more like it,' raged Harry.

'Don't get angry, get even,' said Bob.

'Just give me those bottles of Irish and leave it to me,' said Harry.

The frost from Bob and me was tangible as we boarded the plane, but Harry for some reason was positively gushing to Alfred.

'Let me help you with your bags, old chap, can't have our victor tiring himself out.' He banged on at Alfred all the way over, telling his very worst jokes, so that I began to be sorry for our organiser, perfidious or otherwise.

At Gatwick our voluminous hand luggage got generally

tangled up, and in the confusion Harry must have worked it.

'Just make sure you're ahead of Alfred through customs,' he whispered to us.

The last we saw of Alfred was him waving and hallooing as he was ushered away by two customs officials. Even then Bob saw the gloomy side.

'I suppose they might let him keep the three extra bottles when he explains it all,' he said.

'I don't think so,' said Harry. 'Anyway I shoved a few extra bottles of Vod into the hold-all. The head of customs plays off twenty-two, and he's a stickler for the rules.'

Temperament and Temper

'll break your neck if you say that again.' Not the polite repartee we were used to at St Wilfrid's.

It was a hot day, baking and still, most unusual on those elevated sandhills that make up the ancient links, but I stayed cool.

'You'll miss.'

Like an angry bull, or perhaps bullock, he snorted loudly and clenched his fists, and then with an even louder snort turned on his heels and burst out of the changing rooms and into the corridor that led to the Members' Bar.

'So what?' you may think. Just another tetchy golfer. But there was an important dimension. Club rules are very specific at St Wilfrid's: members and their guests are not allowed into the Members' Bar unless they are wearing a tie. A trivial formality? If only. Not wearing a tie is equivalent at St Wilfrid's to moving your ball in the rough. It didn't matter that the family good looks, such as he possessed, had rather decayed with his sojourn in the Antipodes; but *no tie*?

I had explained all this to brother Archie when he came to play at the hallowed links.

'Whatever they do in Oz,' – I used the colloquial to

appear less pompous, usually a mistake – 'at St Wilfrid's we wear ties. That's the rule, and if you want a drink after the game you'll need a tie.'

'You Brits, it's time you loosened up.'

'Well, that's the rule, and the members keep it.'

'They can keep it, and put it you-know-where. I'm not wearing a tie on my holiday for anyone.'

'You won't get a drink, then.' I sounded perhaps a little smug.

He stomped off to get his clubs, a small brown beer bottle in his left hand. Oh no, I thought, he can't be hitting the sauce already.

So there we were, I making my way to the showers, and my dear brother from Australia tie-less en route for the Members' Bar, the steward, the secretary and perhaps the captain.

When you're having a really good row it's rather like skiing, going a bit faster than you really feel is safe but enjoying it. Only at rest at the bottom do you wonder if you've rather overdone it.

I mused as I stood in the shower that people do get awfully upset on the golf course. I had given Archie a good hiding and he had obviously been disappointed with his game, or rather mine. Ever since he had emigrated he had developed something of a 'Strine strain, and now it had reached hurricane force.

I won't say I didn't feel a sneaking guilt; after all, it was a hot day and I could have got him a drink. But his attitude had annoyed me right from the start, and he was after all lucky to be invited.

'Just because you only come to England once every five years,' I'd said, 'doesn't mean you can ignore our hallowed customs.'

'Stuff your hallowed customs,' he had replied as he got into the car.

I came out of the shower and was a little disappointed to see him standing in the urinals with a pint of lager in his hand. Before I could say anything, he blurted out, 'And don't think I'm going to pay you that fiver after the way you've carried on.'

'And don't think I'm going to invite you to play here again.'

'And don't think I want to play with you here again,' replied Archie, archly.

It probably seems somewhat childish to you, but it gives you some idea how bad-tempered golfers can become. On the course it's a little different: all pumped up, a bundle of nervous anticipation, and someone on a neighbouring tee signals you haven't raked a bunker, which can't be raked anyway because it's rock hard. Perhaps one does overreact.

But a clubhouse argument is something different. All the frustrations you have kept under iron control for eighteen holes suddenly explode in a gush of white fury, like the end of a keg of beer. And if you add to this brotherly love, the mixture is profoundly unstable.

We drove home in silence, and the state of frost was obvious to Celia as we walked in through the front door.

'Well, I hope you two will be getting on better tomorrow.'

'Archie's got to get back to London tonight,' I said sharply.

'No, he has not. I don't care what nonsense you two have been up to, but I've cooked a lovely shoulder of lamb and Archie's going to enjoy it. Aren't you, Archie?'

Archie, despite his conversion to Oz, still had the Englishman's fear of a strong woman.

'If you say so, Celia.'

'Nothing Archie would like more than a bit of lamb. Not the sort of thing they ever see in Australia,' I added wittily.

'And you keep out of this, James. You've caused enough trouble as it is,' carried on Celia. 'Just go and sit down in the living-room and watch a bit of television. You'll never be any good on the course tomorrow if you don't unwind tonight.'

'I'm not playing tomorrow, at least not with your husband.'

There were limits to Archie's fear of Celia, and playing golf with me again was obviously beyond them.

'Yes you are, Archie. I've arranged a nice game for the two of you with Pollard *père et fils* tomorrow morning, and you'll disappoint them very much if you're not there.'

Celia was in full control, but I was confused.

'What are you talking about? You know perfectly well Johnny Douglas and I play on Sunday mornings. Since when was it your business to interfere with my golf? I thought you had your garden.'

'I know exactly what I'm talking about. Paul Pollard has his son down from university and Nancy Pollard rang asking especially if you two would play with them both. You know how much you like Paul and Nancy and it would be a great treat for the youngster.' She added as an afterthought, 'I thought you had some business planned with Paul.'

'I'm glad to say the days are long gone when I have to mix something serious like golf with something trivial like business.' She knew very well my views on the matter but I reminded her anyway.

'His son does play off six, you know.'

'And what about Johnny, since you've arranged everything else?'

'He rang to say he couldn't play tomorrow.'

'He must be going soft in the head,' I said in a low voice as I left the room. Luckily Celia didn't hear.

Only later, sitting in front of the television, did I realise that I now had to ask brother Archie to play. After all, making up a four is one of society's basic obligations and I couldn't see how Archie could refuse. Still, I was apprehensive. Archie had been a long time in Australia.

In fact I was so apprehensive that I said nothing more

about it. I didn't say much at all even over dinner, nor did Archie, but Celia chatted on about her planting plans as though nothing had happened.

'And at the back of the lawn, just before you get to the York stone path that leads to the goldfish pond – do explain it to Archie, Jim – I'm going to put in a new bank of deep golden Japanese azaleas which the garden centre tells me have been specially bred for our climate so they flower in February.'

'Like the Mizugoshi large head offsets,' I muttered.

'What was that, Jim? Are you taking an interest in my garden at last?' said Celia with a touch of steel.

Archie allowed himself the flicker of a smile.

The next morning I decided the best policy was business as usual. It usually is; the policy, that is.

'We're meeting the Pollards at nine.' Pause. 'You'd better make a move,' I shouted through the door of Archie's bedroom. There was no reply. I waited, then banged on the door a couple of times and went downstairs.

I munched through the health-giving muesli and drank a second cup of coffee but there was still no sign of Archie. It was 8:30 and it would take us a quarter of an hour to get down to the course. There was a club match starting at 9:20, so it was important to be prompt.

'Where the hell is he?'

'I don't know, dear. Why don't you go and fetch him?'

'Not likely.'

'Well, you'll be late. I think you're being very childish.'

'Maybe,' I said, standing up.

At that moment the front door slammed and Archie came in from the hall. He was looking flushed and had his little brown beer bottle in his hand. Oh no, I thought.

'Well, are we going to play or aren't we?' he said with the tone of a man who has just sunk a ten-footer.

'You are, Archie, and I hope you slept well,' said Celia. 'Come and have a quick bite before you go.' She was glowing with amusement.

'Don't worry, my superb hostess, I've got all the sustenance I need,' and he waved his beer bottle.

'Really, Archie, you are naughty.'

'I wish you were!'

This was more than I could stand.

'Get in the car, Archie. We're late and we'd like a bit of manners from you.'

'Oh, no improvement on the brotherly front, I see.' He turned to Celia with a jaunty air. 'Wish me luck!'

The Pollards, *père et fils*, were hanging about by the first tee as we rushed up.

'Oh, well done, Jim, you've made it. I think we should be all right if we're quick.'

'Meet my brother Archie, Paul. Archie, this is Paul.'

'Pleased to meet you, Paul,' said Archie, sticking out his hand.

To my great embarrassment he had his beer bottle in it.

There was an awkward moment as Pollard Senior tried to take the hand, and Archie pulled it rapidly away, saying, 'Oh no you don't. I need all the sustenance I can get.'

'I wasn't trying to take your bottle,' said Pollard in confusion.

'I'll give you the benefit of the doubt,' said Archie.

Paul Pollard was a first-rate chap, but I can't say his sense of humour was his strong point. His black bushy eyebrows lowered and he flushed noticeably beneath his weather-beaten visage.

After an awkward silence he turned to me and, beckoning to the tall and sleek young man standing a few yards away, said with obvious pride, 'And this is Peter. He's off six.'

'You'll be much too good,' I said, turning on my best bonhomie, an invaluable golf-club attribute.

There's really nothing more satisfying than a good foursome on a great course. You build up a marvellous swooping rhythm as you eat up the course, punching and counter-punching against competitive but good-humoured opponents. That's what the Pollards had in mind for that morning. It was not to be.

'Archie, this is my son Peter.'

Archie eyed him warily. Peter loped forward, his hand outstretched, his fresh young face wreathed in an innocent smile.

'Like father, like son, eh?' said Archie, putting his beer bottle behind his back.

'Pleased to meet you,' said the boy.

'Likewise,' said Archie. 'Subject to your golf, of course,' he added.

I can't say I was enjoying the encounter up to this point, and I asked myself again why the hell I bothered to entertain my brother, even once every five years. He made cousin Freddy seem really quite amenable. Still, blood is thicker than water, and I have to say there's not much thicker than brother Archie.

'Right, let's get the handicaps sorted out. You're still fourteen, are you not?' said Pollard, turning to me as if he wasn't sure. 'I'm sixteen and rising, and Peter's six.' He obviously couldn't say this often enough. 'What are you off, Archie?'

'The tee,' said Archie.

'Very droll,' said Pollard. 'What's your handicap, old boy?'

'We play each other square,' I answered.

'Well, in that case it's three-eighths of six, which is two, and our honour.' He paused, looked at his son and said with confidence, 'Why don't you show us the way, Peter?'

Peter stepped forward with sublime confidence, pricked the turf with his tee, balanced the ball, stepped back and looked up the fairway, fixing some far distant point, and with a swagger and a wiggle addressed his ball. The silence was tangible. His brow furrowed deeply.

'What are we going to play for?' said Archie.

Pollard Junior put his club down rather sharply and stepped back from the ball. He wore the puzzled frown of a well-trained labrador, unfairly abused. After a silence Pollard Senior made a sort of 'tch' and said, 'Oh, I don't know. What about a fiver a corner?' He winked at his son.

'Fine,' said Archie. 'Presumably on each nine and the match?'

'If you say so,' said Pollard, glancing at Archie's beer bottle.

This time the warm-up went uninterrupted. The lanky boy followed the same routine, reaching a crescendo as he whacked the ball high and long down the middle of the fairway, clearing easily the bank which crosses at about two hundred and thirty yards.

Archie didn't look at me to decide which of us should play, but walked boldly up to the tee, placed his bottle by the white marker and with the least preparation proceeded to attack the ball with real venom. I wouldn't describe his swing as metronomic at the best of times, though I suppose a metronome can go pretty fast if pushed, but on this sunny morning it had more in common with what the sabres must have looked like when the Light Brigade reached the Russian gunners on that fateful day in 1854.

Sheer aggression, total commitment, tremendous power, complete failure. The ball skidded off the end of the tee and buried itself in thick grass ten feet beyond the end of the tee. Archie strode away, his face like thunder, and tossed the club towards his bag.

I will say that Archie didn't take an air shot on those first five holes, but he did everything else. I hung in bravely, but at four down after four for the first nine it's pretty annoying, particularly when your partner appears to have no interest in the game at all. On the fourth I had put him down the middle, but he had contrived to slice it down the bank. I pitched to within twelve feet, admittedly above the hole, and he rolled it down the hill eight feet past. Meanwhile any tension our opponents had had evaporated, and swinging easily they were waltzing round. I actually think I would have got the eight-footer uphill if Archie hadn't bent down to do up his shoelaces just as I played, and so yet again they had two for it.

So on the fifth, when I had a three-footer for a birdie, Archie having fluked a seven-iron, which would at least have kept us in it, I don't blame myself for sliding it by. I do blame Archie for missing the three-footer back.

Both Pollards were now full of good humour. You might have thought they would have resented that we weren't giving them much of a match; not a bit of it. It was all, 'Hard luck.' – 'So close.' – 'Well tried.' – 'Only another few feet,' and so on, the full panoply of patronising twaddle.

Archie himself continued round in his nightmare, his face black with discontent, his shoulders hunched in a furious determination which only seemed to make him play worse.

'Well, that's the first nine,' said Pollard. 'How about another fiver on the bye, the last thirteen?'

'Well, maybe—' I began.

'Yes,' said Archie with a vicious edge to his voice.

The next four holes were uneventful, except for one small ray of hope. Pollard Junior drew his ball a little too much on the ninth, partly as a result of taking the wrong line, and his father said, 'Steady now.' The young athlete didn't seem too pleased by this advice and fluffed his chip after his father had dug him out of the pot bunker. So we were only five down in the match and all square on the bye at the turn.

Any worries the father-and-son team may have had were dispelled by the sight of Archie making off to the car park at the turn and coming back with another small beer bottle. Junior smirked and Senior winked back.

'Getting refreshments, eh?'

'Yes,' said Archie, 'and don't tell me it's illegal. I know it is, but this is a friendly, isn't it?'

'Quite so,' said Paul Pollard sententiously.

I can't really say where the turning point came. There were quite a few, I suppose, a series of little swings which kept us in the match. Archie's second at the tenth to within five feet, which I sank for a change, was obviously a goodly blow. I think the Pollards were too enthusiastic about our birdie, patronisingly so.

At the next Archie had a ten-footer for par. Just as he was going to play he stopped and turned to the boy wonder and said severely, 'Please don't move when I'm about to play.'

I must say I hadn't seen the boy move, but he reddened and said sorry.

'Don't give it another thought, sport,' said Archie.

Archie sank the putt, and the boy missed his five-footer. We were two up on the back nine. On the next I put us off to the right and father Pollard was off to the left. Son was about to play when Archie bellowed, 'It's me to play!' He then addressed the ball with a furious intensity and heaved his body at it. 'Bloody hell!' he shouted almost at once.

'Where did it go?' I asked.

'God knows,' he said loudly.

Rather surprisingly, when we reached the green our ball was about fifteen feet from the flag and they had found the right-hand bunker. Father splashed out to within twenty feet, and now Archie took the chance to congratulate him.

'Practically cold,' he said.

They two-putted and we won our third hole in succession.

For some reason this was a cue for my brother to be a little more forthcoming.

'Jeez, I'm playing badly,' he said, 'but it's a superb course and a great day to be out in the open.'

These remarks didn't receive quite the glow they would have done earlier in the round. I must admit the Pollards were getting a bit testy.

At the thirteenth I hit rather a good three-iron into the

wind over the sandhill. Pollard Senior pressed and fell short into the long grass beside the path on the down slope.

'Too many baked beans,' said Archie.

'What?' said Pollard.

'Wind,' said Archie.

Pollard turned away.

I felt that it was up to me to restore the good humour with which we had begun the round, but I couldn't see how.

'Come on, Archie, no jokes, please,' I said lamely. 'I hope he's not putting you off,' I said to the son.

'No,' he replied through gritted teeth.

We halved the fourteenth, thanks to the boy missing from four feet, and our opponents stalked off in less than perfect harmony. I heard the father say, 'You're too fast on the back-swing,' but I didn't catch the reply. It's never easy to give one's partner constructive advice, especially if it's your own son.

At the fifteenth tee the boy was swishing his driver in anticipation like an angry dragonfly. Archie ambled up and sat down on the bench.

After a moment or two the boy said peevishly, 'Your honour.'

'Just coming, just coming.' Archie got out his beer bottle and had a swig. 'I'm bushed,' he said.

'The club match will be catching us up soon,' said Pollard Senior.

'Oh my word, we can't have that,' said Archie and, springing up like a jack-rabbit, went straight to the tee and without a practice swing crashed it down the middle. 'Not bad for a quick swipe, eh?' he said as he left the tee.

It's a strange thing, but if the most relaxed willowy swing – the poetry of golf – loses its timing, it suddenly looks gangling and incompetent, a broken reed. This happened to poor Peter now.

He hit a weak slice which ballooned up and lodged itself in the long grass just before the pump hut. Pollard Senior dug at it without conviction. I put ours fairly stiff and they conceded the hole. We had now won the bye and the back nine, and were one up in the match.

'What's the score?' asked Archie.

Pollard Senior almost spat it out.

'Exciting!' said Archie. 'Shall we have something on the bye-bye?'

'No,' said the Pollards in unison, a revival of the team spirit which had not been much in evidence recently. In fact it was the last flutter. We reached the seventeenth dormie, and they had every appearance of lambs to the slaughter. As it happened there was a bit of fight left.

Archie had a six-footer for our par three. He missed it, but gone was his monosyllabic mien of early in the round. Rather he gave a loud curse, followed up by: 'How could you, you berk! You've played like a moron, moron, moron!' He continued muttering and banging his putter head against the ground.

Poor Peter stood over his four-footer, Archie still banging his club on the ground. Then he suddenly rounded on Archie.

'Just stop that, will you? You've been putting me off all the way round. You're just a bloody cheat. And a drunk.'

It was all rather hysterical.

There was a bit of a silence, then Pollard Senior broke in, very clear and cool: 'Peter, apologise or never play on this course again.'

There was another long pause, during which all I could hear was Archie banging his putter head on the ground.

'No,' said Peter, with an attempt to match the cold steel of his father. Then he threw his putter on the ground, picked up his clubs and walked off towards the clubhouse.

Pollard Senior fished in his bag for the twenty quid he owed us, handed it over silently, shook hands and walked off after his son, picking up the discarded putter on the way. Not a happy man.

'Some people take golf much too seriously,' mused Archie, tossing his beer bottle into a bush.

I really don't approve of litter, so I retrieved the bottle. To my surprise the beer was non-alcoholic.

Choosing the Line

After I married Celia and she took up gardening, I realised that the two sports were properly separated. It was therefore more from a matter of nostalgia that I followed Joe's suggestion of partnering his lady wife in the President's Mixed Foursomes. You may ask what sort of a B.F. Joe must be to have asked me, but I can quite see his point of view. Miriam, despite her somewhat archaic name, was and probably is a very modern woman; and when he persuaded her to take up golf, I can quite see her acquiescence demanded some countervailing sacrifice from him. As it happened, and as you know it often does, when the lady wife actually took up the game she had all the natural talent that Joe lacked. The question was temperament; Joe's.

'Listen, Jim, you would be doing me, and of course Miriam, an awful favour if you would consider partnering her for the President's Mixed Foursomes this year.'

'Come, come,' I said in my most expansive way, 'you've come on such a lot, Joe. I can't believe that Miriam wouldn't want to put herself at your mercy.'

'Thanks, Jim,' he agonised, 'but the truth is I simply can't face it. Of course I can drive all right, even my short irons hold up, but there is something beyond flesh and blood in having your own wife watch you putt.'

145

He paused and I knew what he was going to add; it came back to me in painfully cruel relief. 'Especially when she putts better than you do,' I said, laughing.

'Yes,' he answered gloomily, and then with some heat added, 'not that she does, really. It's just that awful intensity that she looks at me with, when I've got a four-footer. It reminds me of the way she looks at the washing-up. Why the hell should I sink it? I ask myself. And then I don't, and she gives me a pained expression.'

'There are some clubs which simply don't recognise women as existing. They can play, so long as they don't mind being hit on the head. A fair compromise, really.'

He was not to be distracted. 'Listen, Jim, please will you play with Miriam? You'll make me happy, you'll make her happy, you may even make yourself happy – up to a point, at any rate.'

I was rather shocked by his determination, but I rose to the occasion.

'Of course I will, Joe. Tell Miriam to give me a call. It'll be a pleasure.' I was positively moved by Joe's sigh of relief.

Miriam is a mousy woman who could be called petite, or even gamine, but to stick with the English she becomes on the golf course a mighty mouse, a bionic mouse. As I watched the miniature elegance of her game I felt sorry for her; what a golfer she would have made as a man.

As requested, she rang me that Sunday evening. I let it ring, wondering who it might be, thinking it might be

Miriam, waiting for Celia to do the needful, but my heart beating a little faster none the less.

'It's Miriam Fry for you, Jimmy. She says you're expecting her to ring about golf.' As she handed me the phone she added, 'You might have answered.'

'Oh, yes, I forgot she was going to ring.'

The rather nervous but crisp voice addressed me. 'It's Miriam Fry speaking. Joe said you would partner me in the foursomes.'

I could feel myself smiling, I suppose with pride. 'Of course, Miriam, how nice of you to want to.'

'Are you sure you'd like to? I mean, my game is improving but it's a long way to go.'

'We're all pygmies on the golf course,' I said. No insult was intended and I don't believe any was taken, but I suppose I could have chosen my words better.

Playing with a woman, as I had discovered in those early days with Celia, is different from playing with a man. Not just the start of the whole thing, though the camaraderie in the locker room beforehand is quite different. The segregation of the sexes means that you don't stumble over your partner looking for your second golf shoe, or his dazed-looking head coming out of a basin of cold water, but rather you search with some trepidation on the putting green, which has become more reminiscent of the teenage dance floor. And the locker-room conversation is rather different, too, though I'm glad to say at St Wilfrid's the coarser innuendo is not encouraged.

'Hello, Miriam, lovely morning,' I shouted across the green swathe as I saw her sink a ten-footer, a nice steady pendulum stroke. I know enough to avoid the merest whiff of condescension with a golfing woman.

'Oh, there you are, Jim, I was beginning to wonder about you.'

'No need, I wouldn't have missed this morning for anything,' I blurted out gauchely. The truth was I had a new theory about putting practice. It put you off if you missed a lot on the practice green, while it gave you a false sense of confidence if you sank everything, so I was experimenting with no practice at all.

'You've got time for a few practice putts,' she said. I acquiesced.

On the tee the gents played off first. Tommy, the male of our opponents, said gallantly, 'Mugs away,' and proceeded to carve it up into the long grass above the ninth.

His partner was a hatchet-faced woman of about fifty-five called Penny. She rasped out, 'Hard lines.'

To my surprise I got away with mine. Not the ideal shot, in fact it could have been disastrous, but thinned and cut it ran low to the left, got a good kick right and left Miriam well perched on the top of the bank which commands the long plane running up to the first.

'Well, I got away with it,' I said with some relief, forestalling the congratulations.

'Yes,' said Miriam.

No frills on that, I thought to myself.

Choosing the Line

There's a certain sort of tennis partner who says nothing but just plays. None of this 'Sorry, partner, it had a bad bounce', 'Sorry, partner, there's that damn fly again.' They just play their best and shut up. Well, Miriam was that sort of partner.

On that first she hit a perfectly formed three wood which went on about 140 yards. I cried out, 'Beautifully hit, partner!'

She slightly inclined her head.

I put our third stiff from about a hundred yards.

She noted my achievement with a slight incline of her left eyebrow.

What a woman! I thought.

With that attitude we couldn't really lose, and we didn't.

It was over the G & T in the bar, or maybe the way she stroked the ball into the hole from eight feet on the sixteenth to clinch the match, that I began to develop that awful crawling feeling up the back of my spine, or somewhere like that, that came with the unpleasant recognition that there was more to Miriam than just her golf.

If you see a woman in brown brogues, a sensible tweed skirt and a headscarf you may think all sorts of things, but wearing the same attire on a golf tee, save that the headscarf is replaced by a sensible tam-o-shanter and her hair is in a pony-tail, then she must be allowed to enter the portals of the golfer and leave her womanhood behind. At least, that's always been my attitude.

'You hit the ball sweetly today, Jimmy,' she said, putting her hand on my knee.

'Thanks, partner, can I get you another G & T?'

'I really must get back.'

'Joe will understand. One more and then I'll drop you off.'

Once the tectonic plates have shifted, they cannot unshift: no longer mousy, nothing less than very cute. As far as I was concerned our relationship was now on that slippery slope, and there was nothing I could either do or say to stop it. In that instant, offering her a lift home, I imagined myself to have crossed a personal Rubicon. I had changed from the perfectly honed golfing machine (well, almost) to the creeping cougar stalking its prey.

The drive home was largely uneventful. 'I think that next Saturday's opponents may be a tougher proposition.'

'We'll just have to play our best,' she said contentedly.

I followed up with some talk of tactics, and she appeared to listen carefully. 'I think it might be worth planning our holes a little more carefully,' I said as we drew up to her driveway. Perhaps subconsciously I remembered my first evening with Celia.

'Good idea, Jim, let's meet in the bar for a coffee before the game.'

'Fine,' I said, keeping the disappointment out of my voice.

'Here we are. Come in and say hello to Joe.'

'Thank you, but I can't stay long. Celia's expecting me.'

'How did it go?' asked Celia that evening.

'Fine,' I said.

'Not falling for the charms of Mrs Fry, I hope.'

'Don't be silly, dear,' I said in an effort for light-heartedness which I suspect sounded a bit leaden.

As was usual for me during the week, I mentally re-lived the game of the previous weekend as I sat behind my desk in the office, or motored home down the leafy lanes in the evening, but this week into my careful analysis kept dropping a visual image of Mrs Fry, and the peculiar neatness of her well-balanced swing.

Next Saturday the wind was high and the conditions tough. We met as planned for coffee and as I looked at her small frame, delicately balancing the cup in her porcelain fingers, I wondered how she would withstand the buffets of the southwester. Over coffee I set out my plan, a very much more sophisticated version of the one that had so very nearly succeeded with me and Celia years before. The essence as before was to play short and chip dead. She listened with absolute silence, so occasionally I repeated myself. At the end she smiled sweetly and said she thought these sorts of chats were very good for the nerves.

'You will play to the plan, won't you?' I asked urgently.

'Let's just say I'll do my best,' and she put her hand on my knee for the second time in our relationship, so I could hardly complain.

I played a blinder. As for her ability to withstand the southwester I need not have worried. Despite her frailty she stood her ground and swung with the same calm confidence I so much admired. It was a thoroughly enjoyable day's canter over the eighteen, only spoilt by old Alfred, organiser of our memorable holiday to Ireland and my opponent of the morning, saying in the showers afterwards, 'Well, you certainly seem to have clicked with Miriam.'

'Oh, do you think so?' I asked naively.

'Obviously. You beat us four and three.'

'Oh, yes, of course.' I hoped I hadn't given myself away, but Alfred gave a leer.

'What did you think I meant?'

'I didn't think you meant anything,' I snapped, drying myself quickly.

'I should reward you,' she said as I dropped her off.

'Your golf is my reward. You really are the perfect partner.'

'You're such a gentleman, Jim, and you're forgetting my putt on the seventh.'

'It's a horrible green, and anyway I was lucky with the return.'

She waited a moment, her hand on the door.

'You know, Miriam, I think we really have a chance in this competition.'

She smiled particularly sweetly. 'Yes?'

'Don't you think it would be worth putting in a little extra practice?' I paused. 'What about Wednesday evening?'

'Good idea.' She was her most matter-of-fact again.

That Wednesday I explained to Celia where I was going.

'Taking Miriam rather seriously, aren't you?' she said.

'I'd much rather be playing with you, Celia,' said I.

I arrived at the practice ground to see a little beige figure in the distance. In the long shadows of early summer I could see the strange stride of a Giacometti figure with a beautifully finished if elongated five-iron. It had a certain perfection which I relish to remember.

'Where have you been?' she said, when at last we were united over her fifty practice balls.

We hit a couple of full bags each and I waited patiently for her to flag. At last it was I who said, 'Well, I've shanked the last three, I think it's time to go. How about a drink?'

'Isn't Celia expecting you?'

'Not for a while. I said we'd probably talk tactics after we'd finished.'

'Good. You do like your tactics, don't you?'

I looked at her sharply but she seemed quite serious.

153

Over a G & T in the town we did talk tactics, until I asked what I must admit was intended to be a leading question. 'How on earth did you get interested in this frightful game, anyway?'

There are certain things you don't joke about and I had discovered the threshold.

'It may be frightful to you, but in that case I don't know why you spend so much effort on it.'

I think of myself as a rather sensitive type, but at that moment I saw within that calfskin golf glove a Harry Vardon grip of steel. The reply I had prepared – 'To spend time with you' – froze on my lips and I replied weakly, 'Of course I take it seriously. I was only joking.'

For the third time in our relationship she put her hand on my knee.

'Please don't joke about it, Jim.'

I dropped her home shortly afterwards, both of us thoughtful, I deep in admiration.

Anyway, we gelled. Her studied calm and her absolute reliability matched my tactical cunning and length off the tee, and we moved through the field like a knife through butter. In the clubhouse the Fry–South combo was attracting favourable comment. We gave the impression of utter professionalism which is so intimidating to the amateur golfer.

And that professionalism could only be achieved for my part by putting out of my mind any thought of Miriam as woman. The creeping cougar had been put back in his cage. I was the absolute master of my emotions.

I do have to admit that, as I played, my mind occasionally wandered from the mechanical excellence of her follow-through to consideration of its sheer beauty, but I had conquered the childish infatuation I had felt at the beginning of our golfing relationship.

The other fancied team was a mother–son combination, the Ryder-Smiths from Horley. Ryder-Smith *mère* was a fine woman in her mid-fifties with a voice trained for the command of dogs and children, while her son Randy would have made a superb flying ace, or at least acted like one. His golf reflected this, an amusing mixture of swoops out of the sun, let down by the occasional prang of monumental proportions.

We made an odd foursome as we strode off down the first in the semi-final of the President's Mixed Foursomes. If I hadn't been playing with Miriam, I would have laughed out loud at the sight of Ryder-Smith *père*, like a lugubrious butler, solemnly pulling the trolley for *mère* while young Randy swished his three wood like the young hero he imagined himself to be. After three months of golf with Miriam, however, the one thing I knew not to do was to cough, let alone laugh. It did help to keep the concentration.

The match was a cracker, punch and counter-punch of the highest order. Young Randy cracking the ball well over the bank on the first, and his mother sinking a birdie putt. I chipping dead from Old Man's Ditch on the second. Miriam perching our ball with precision on the convex fairway of the fourth. I threading my three wood between the bunkers on the sixth.

We came to the eighteenth level. The excitement was intense, and for the first and last time in our golfing relationship I took Miriam's hand in mine as we walked up the small rise to the eighteenth tee.

'Solidly on the fairway as planned,' I whispered. To my surprise her grip was fierce, and I thought of her hand on my knee.

She hit a beauty, short and straight. La Ryder-Smith outhit her but it rolled off to the right into some long grass. I hit our second well, but the wind was from the south-west and we were still seventy yards short. Randy took a five wood out of the rough and hit a high ballooning ball into the chasm on the right. I punched my hand into my fist in an unsporting gesture. Miriam smiled, to my surprise. *Mère* put the ball back on the fairway and Randy hit a solid ball on to the green, twenty-five feet from the flag. They looked a certainty for a six.

'Just roll it up, two putts and we're home.'

Miriam didn't look at me but squared up carefully. Her approach was well hit but had a little more backspin than she expected, leaving me a very long putt, uphill from the front of the green across a slope. I hit it pretty well, but there was still a four-footer.

To my horror Ryder-Smith *mère* proceeded to roll in her monster for a five, and now the pressure was on Miriam.

I suppose it was my fault. Why didn't I keep my big mouth shut? 'It's only a game.'

The sentiment was banal, but it stopped her short. She looked at me, her eyes blazing. She was about to speak and then she bit it back, but she stood looking at me. Even today I don't know what she thought, what she would have said, but she was clearly caught in indecision. Anyway, it wasn't the frame of mind in which to hit a putt, and she missed.

These gender stereotypes are rather ridiculous, I suppose, but no one can pretend Miriam was a good loser.

'Well played, Ryder-Smiths,' I said firmly.

I think Miriam said something more muted, but more to the point she added, 'Please don't wait for me in the bar. We have some people coming over and I must get back.'

'I'll run you back, partner. Hold on.'

The air was heavy in the car as we left the pebbles of the car park and I turned on to the well-cambered fenland road which took us back to the ancient town.

As I drove I considered opening after opening which might break the spell that had come over us, the lowering dark clouds of depression which can so easily weigh down the defeated. We had never lost before and the Fry–South combo was doom-laden.

157

At last we reached the Frys' drive and I pulled up. I had to say something.

'There's more to life than golf, I say,' putting my hand on her knee. To my absolute horror I saw that her eyes were glazed; she was looking straight ahead and a tear ran down her right cheek.

Luckily, at that moment Joe came round the corner of the house. 'How did it go?' he shouted.

'Not too well,' I replied, in what I think was reasonable understatement. Miriam's head was in her handbag. When it emerged the sun was once more shining.

'Well, you must enter again next year,' said Joe with as much good humour as could be mustered.

'Absolutely,' I said.

Miriam made no comment at that moment, but digging in the boot for her clubs she said to me, quietly but emphatically, 'What would be the point?'

I still haven't worked that out, but I did decide mixed foursomes were not for me. It's all too emotional.

Outrageous Fortune

'I hope he was fully insured,' said Robert somewhat wistfully.

'Oh, I should think so,' said I. 'If it's who I think it is.'

'Not the insurance salesman himself?'

'The very one.'

It was an extraordinary coincidence. Here we were, guests at this great Surrey club, playing an afternoon round. We had been approached by a member over pre-lunch drinks. He introduced himself as Trevor Brown and tried to sell us insurance, in a not-very-subtle manner. And now Robert seemed to have picked him off.

'It would be him.' Gazing into the pines to the left, Robert added, 'Serves him right.'

'Really, he wasn't such a bad sort, just a bit pushy. Anyway,' I said with some relish, 'it's not his insurance that's at issue, it's yours. Permanent disability at least, compensation to widow and dependants more likely.'

'He must be covered for all that.'

'Of course, but the wife – or widow – will be able to throw the lot at you.'

'It's a fine thing when a game of golf involves more lawyers than a corporate takeover.'

'Well, maybe you should take some advice on how to drive straight.'

'I only hit him a glancing blow. And he shouldn't have been lurking about in those trees. He must have hit an awful tee shot off the thirteenth.'

We had seen the figure emerge from the shadow of the pines after Robert had hit a long curling hook, clutch his head, reel slightly and then fall on to his face.

'It didn't look particularly glancing to me,' I rejoined. The seriousness of the situation began to dawn.

'You'd better go to the clubhouse, Jim, and get a doctor. I'll see what I can do about our friend.' And he strode off into the long grass. I cannot describe him better than as the image of a golfer in search of a badly hit ball.

As I made my way back down to the first at a gentle trot, the horror of it all loomed ever larger. I went puffing along and the words of the poet ran heavily through my head – *To every man upon this earth/Death cometh soon or late.* But the next lines seemed curiously inappropriate – *And how can man die better/Than facing fearful odds/For the ashes of his fathers/And the temples of his gods?*

I suppose you could say that the salesman was facing pretty fearful odds, rooting around for his ball to the right of the thirteenth green when Robert, with his fearful hook, was about to drive from the second. On the other hand you could say his odds were quite good. After all, balls zing over the courses of our fair and pleasant land all weekend and remarkably few people get brought low. Golfers haven't taken to the helmet of the batting crease, not out of any greater bravery but because the odds are substantially better.

I was musing to this effect when I hurtled – or rather, staggered breathlessly – up the stairs of the great club and choked out to a member coming out of the bar, 'Someone's been hit.'

'Hard luck,' said the member, and left.

I realised that, at this particular club, as far as members were concerned it was *sauve qui peut*, so I presumed the secretary was given sole charge. I accosted the next member between exhausted gasps. 'Where's the secretary?'

'No idea. Maybe in his room.' And he too sauntered out.

I eventually found the secretary's room, a model of its type. Old golfing prints, postcards stuck to a pinboard, lists of members and handicaps, last year's fixtures, annotated, a computer clearly set aside for use by a skilled operative, the secretary's old chair, old wood, well used, and a pipe on its side in a battered ashtray. Hardly the tautly coiled spring of the modern office, but a place where the various compromises necessary to any great club could be conceived and the letters written to bring those compromises about. I have to say that it seems to me that the work done by the secretary is far more effective over the G & T, or two, than anything committed to paper.

I looked round in mild admiration at the rightness of it all before really taking in that the room was empty. I thought of Robert cradling Trevor the insurance man in his arms, perhaps giving him the kiss of life while his spirit ebbed away, and I was re-energised. I rushed into the main bar.

'Have you seen the secretary?' I asked the barman.

'Who wants him?'

'There's a man dying on the course.'

'You think it's the secretary?'

'No,' I replied, a little taken aback.

'Well, what's it to do with him, then?'

I was puzzled for a moment but retrieved myself with, 'It's a member.'

'Why didn't you say so?' And quick as Jack Flash he went round the bar and led me through to the billiard room, adding over his shoulder with some acerbity, as though I was responsible, 'He wouldn't want to miss a thing like that.'

The secretary, despite his age, did react with surprising vigour. 'A dying member? Well, well, well. Take me to him at once.'

'He's in the long rough to the left of the second.'

'Good, we should be able to get there by car. Come round the back.'

We sat in the large, vintage Rover as he turned over the engine. It didn't start at once. 'Oh, damn. I had a new distributor head fitted the other day and it's been a problem ever since.' He knocked his pipe off against the ashtray. 'Did you say he was dying, or dead?'

'Dying, I think.'

'Well, we must get a move on then.'

'Perhaps we should take my car,' I volunteered.

'Certainly not, old man. If a secretary can't go to a member in distress, what good is he?'

The car choked into life and I was spared an answer.

'Death on the course is not as rare as you might think,' the secretary opined as the great motor rolled out of the club drive and stalled as it reached the public road.

'There are more ways of dying on a golf course than being out at cricket, and like cricket it's hard to remember all of them.' He was in a happy mood as we started off again. 'At a great links course, St Wilfrid's, for example, members go down like flies during the winter months. The secretary there once told me he thought they did it on purpose. You couldn't put your overcoat down without some late member being laid out on it, and you didn't get it back until the ambulance arrived. Used to impress the girls, of course. Sailing the South Atlantic on the *Kon-Tiki* may have seemed like something, but departing this world while crossing the rise at the thirteenth into the face of a winter gale, well, that's real endurance.'

'Or lack of it,' I said under my breath.

'What's that?'

'Nothing.'

'Ever been to St Wilfrid's?'

'I'm a member, actually.'

'Oh, really,' he said with disapproval. Clearly standards had fallen.

'Most of the members here prefer to die in bed,' he continued in the same tone. I looked for the hint of a smile, but could find none.

As we reached the road which crossed the second from right to left he asked, 'Heart attack, I suppose?'

'No, actually, he was hit by a ball.'

'Ah ha!'

'A long curling hook off the second.'

'Ah ha!' He paused. 'And who was it?'

'Robert Thorogood.'

'Robert Thorogood? But he's not a member.'

'No, you gave us permission to play.'

'I thought you said a member had been hit?'

'He has been.' I spoke slowly and clearly. 'By Robert Thorogood.'

He became quite grumpy. 'Well, you may have had permission to play, but this seems to be going rather far. Killing a member, eh?'

I began to get the giggles. I don't usually giggle, but the situation was conducive to it.

'Pull yourself together, man.' The secretary took a gentler tone. Perhaps he thought I was crying. 'These things happen. Come on, let's find the body.'

At that moment we saw Robert, alone under the pines, mooching about disconsolately. He put his arms out to either side as we approached him, reminding me of the scene on the seventeenth in the Founder's Foursome the year before, when he couldn't find our ball though it had landed at his feet, and we were well placed to go into the next round.

'I can't find him.'

'What?' the secretary bellowed.

'He's not here.'

The secretary looked at me, his eyes heavy with accusation. I felt responsible, but the hilarity of it all overcame me again as I choked out, 'He must be here, Robert, we saw him go down.'

'The rough is awfully deep,' said Robert in resignation.

'Come, come, man, it's not elephant grass. You can't lose a body in it,' said the secretary.

'I'll go back to the tee and give you the line,' I said and trotted up the path through the heather.

At this point a four-ball appeared at the tee. They had that collective mien of golfers bristling that is peculiar to a four-ball when it is about to be held up. Before I was able to explain, the smallest of the four, in a yellow jersey and tartan trews, said, 'Mind if we play through.'

It was a statement, not a question, implying, if you do mind I don't care.

'I'm not playing, or not at the moment.' I tried to explain. 'There's a dead man up there.'

'Where?'

'Well, we're not quite sure. I'm trying to get the line.'

I looked at their faces; the bristling had given way to an uneasy truce between apoplexy and disbelief. I bit my tongue hard as another wave of laughter came over me, but this time I couldn't contain it and I had to sit down. The tears flowed freely and I howled.

'Pull yourself together,' said the largest of the four. 'Was he a friend of yours?'

'Look, the secretary's waving,' said another. 'He's up there in the rough.'

'I think he's waving us through,' said the tartan trews, who bustled forward with his driver. He had a quick but perfectly oiled swing, and before I could draw breath for another bout of choking he had whacked his ball high up the fairway.

At that moment the sound of sirens filled the Surrey woods and, through my tears, I saw the flashing blue lights of an ambulance. It tore off the road and came down the second fairway, everyone waving. Tartan Trews' drive hit its front mudguard and bounced off into the rough on the other side. To my surprise the ambulance didn't stop at the pines, or at least only briefly, but came right up to the second tee, bouncing and spinning through the heather, the siren screaming.

The ambulancemen were out in a trice, carrying the inevitable red blanket, and it was a moment's work for them to throw it round my shoulders and start to help me into the back of the vehicle. The only impediment

to their progress was Tartan Trews complaining vora-
ciously, 'I've never seen such poor course manners. I'll
be writing to St John's.'

It was just as well Robert turned up at that point.

'You can't do that to Jim,' he shouted in my defence.

'Stand clear, sir, he's had a nasty shock.'

'Maybe, but you can't take him away, he's my partner.'

'Your course manners are the worst I've ever seen,'
repeated the Trews.

'Stand back now, he needs air.'

'No he doesn't, he needs to get back on the course,'
said Robert.

'He's been hit, sir.'

'No, he hasn't,' said Robert.

'He hasn't been,' confirmed the secretary, struggling
up.

'He should have been,' said Trews.

'He's in a right state,' determined the ambulancemen.
'We'll take him in for observation.'

At last I regained my strength and, struggling free,
confronted the ambulancemen. 'You certainly won't take
me in. We're halfway through a round.'

The ambulancemen at last stood back. Luckily they
were golfers.

'In the middle of a round, eh? That's different, then. It
wouldn't do to disturb a round.'

And they got back in the wagon and, lights still flashing,
reeled off down the fairway at great speed.

I suppose we could have held our place on the course, but the four-ball were all members, and a moment of relaxation to restore our calm seemed in order. The secretary took the opportunity to recover his pomposity.

'I would ask you to make a full report when you return to the clubhouse. I think you owe the club a convincing explanation of this extraordinary set of circumstances. I may be forced to write to St Wilfrid's.'

Both secretary and members seemed extraordinarily proud of their ability to write.

We had a reasonable round, not great. I hit a beautiful drive on the short par-four ninth, almost driving the green, almost sinking the chip across the two-tier green and anyway getting one back on Robert with my birdie. After the tenth, when I was on in two with an excellent three wood, admittedly with the wind behind, I was in with a chance, being only one down.

But then we came to the hut. No, not the name of a hole but literally a hut where the members revived their flagging spirits. A perfectly reasonable idea if one was playing bowls or suchlike, but for a game which depends on rhythm I find it quite extraordinary. Anyway, the match rather petered out after the hut and Robert was a relatively easy winner. I forget the exact score.

When we got back to the clubhouse there was quite a crowd in the main bar. The Members' Bar was for once deserted and there was an air of expectancy as we walked in, Robert with a slightly irritating swagger, reflecting the seventy-nine he claimed.

Silence fell, and in the crowd sitting facing us like an examining magistrate sat not the secretary but Trev, the insurance salesman, with his head in a bandage.

'Well, gents, surprised to see me? Alive, that is?'

'No, not really,' said Robert coolly. 'We couldn't find your body so we presumed you must be in the bar.' He paused and added somewhat gratuitously, 'Sold any policies?'

I thought there would be a nasty scene, but for once Robert had read the mood just right. Gales of laughter followed his remark. 'Not yet, but he's still trying!' 'You had second thoughts, by any chance?' Suchlike were hollered out by the company.

Robert offered to buy Trevor a drink, who winked at the barman and said, 'The usual, Sam,' and after a while he unwound the bandage, revealing a pristine scalp free of bumping or bruising.

Robert continued to take the whole thing in good heart, even including the secretary in a round, who seemed as irritated with Trevor as with Robert. I saw his point, and was a little shocked at how effective the pink gin proved at restoring his good humour.

For my part I regarded it as a thoroughly silly joke, and a reminder if one was needed not to stray too far from one's home club.

The Hell of Putting

We were sitting in the club-
house after a pretty satisfying round of golf. At least, it
had been pretty, if not entirely satisfying. The views from
St Wilfrid's on the south-east tip of England are spec-
tacular. They stretch across St Wilfrid's Bay towards
Mallory Cliffs to the west and over Henry's Marsh to the
east. The view inland is dominated by the town of St
Wilfrid's, once a medieval port, almost a Cinque Port,
now a living museum, the greying of England. The river
Ringer curls down past Ringer Sands, amongst which
the eighteen holes of golf make their tantalising way.

Tantalising; that is the essence of golf. As we idly chatted about our rounds over further rounds of bitter, we
waxed quite philosophical on the nature of the irritation
we felt crawling beneath the surface of a game of golf.
The wind had been high, so much so that our lips tasted
salty and my glasses were slightly misted. The rollers
had been visible some way out to sea, as the incoming
tide had met the sandbanks which ribbed the side of the
bay and had been slowly submerged as our round had
progressed.

As we philosophised, aesthetics had only been the leit-
motif of our discussion. Indeed, aesthetics had played a
small part in one hole, the fourth. My ball had lodged at
the foot of some daffodils. It was an isolated clump and

set off most sweetly the swathe of the fairway against the rising bank of rough sandy ground which I had to clear to reach the green. I was about to play it, certain to take the blooms with the ball, when one of my opponents suggested I moved the ball, not nearer the hole, without penalty. This was clearly in contravention of the rules of golf but I nevertheless agreed, a triumph of aesthetics over ethics. Incidentally, my opponents also won a small psychological victory, since I duffed the ball into the rising ground ahead.

It was not over such relatively minor traumas that we philosophised; no, it was the heart of the tantalising game that held our attention – putting. In particular, why a beautiful day, with good company and some not-too-strenuous exercise in delightful surroundings, could be so totally kiboshed by a missed short putt.

To non-golfers the 'missed short putt' may seem rather trivial. Why should it be any more galling to fail to hit a ball three or four feet into a hole than to hook a ball into a ravine off a little wooden peg?

'It's because it ought to be so simple,' said Alfred, with an accountant's certainty. 'A landlady on Bognor sea-front would be able to do it with a little practice. That's why it makes us all so mad.'

'Yes, but could she do it under pressure?' I asked. 'After all, you can't practise pressure. You either cope with it or you don't.'

'Exactly!' barked Bob, removing his pipe. 'You, I dare

say even I, take the whole thing too damned seriously for our own good. I'm sure those old Scots played to inject a bit of competition into a pleasant walk.'

'And spoil it, too!' chipped in Harry. 'Just think how much happier we'd all be if we never missed those short little bastards.'

There was no denying it. It did spoil the day a bit. We pulled on our pints and mulled over the thought. I stared into the dark gold liquid, its froth almost gone, and thought just how wonderful it would be never to miss another short putt. Nothing less than four feet would do fine. What wouldn't I give?

'What wouldn't I give never to miss from four feet or less,' I said.

'What wouldn't you give?' asked Harry.

I smiled. 'I'd give anything. Just think how marvellous it would be.' I pursed my lips and said it again. 'I'd give anything.'

Silence reigned, and for a moment I felt a little peculiar. Would I really give anything? Would I be like Faustus and give my soul, my after-life? Well, I'm not a particularly religious sort of chap, but I suppose we all have our superstitions. Perhaps I'd said more than I'd really meant, but then people say things like that all the time, don't they?

Anyway, we supped up our drinks and with cheery goodnights made our respective ways home. Next week it was the monthly medal, and we'd hardly bothered to say 'See you next week' since it was so inevitable.

'How did it go, darling?' asked Celia over supper.

'Fine, thanks. I played quite well.' The conversation was largely conventional.

'You are a fanatic, but I suppose you're harmless with it.' This was her normal line.

'Yes, darling. I just wish I didn't miss those short putts.'

'Well, don't.'

'Good idea.' I paused. 'How's the mulching getting on?'

'It's the wrong time of year.'

'Surely not.'

'Well, not ideal.'

'I thought mulching was like golf – a year-round activity.'

'Not really.' I found it hard to relate to Celia's interest in gardening.

Next Sunday was much like the previous one, another high wind from the south-west, coolish with sunny periods punctuated by showers. A difficult day for golf, especially difficult for putting on the ice-like greens on which St Wilfrid's rightly prides itself.

I will not take you through it hole by hole; non-golfers would find it hard to follow. Golfers would be surprised by my ability to hook, pull, slice, thin, push and top in the course of a morning. I like to think I know how to work a course. Certainly recovery shots are an important part of my repertoire. Still, the point is that my round worked out pretty well, or rather more than that. In fact, when all the cards were in, I'd won the monthly medal for the first time.

'Good show, Jim. I hear you were deadly on the greens,' said Bob over a kümmel after lunch.

'Hardly. I sank a twelve-footer on the third and about an eight-footer on the thirteenth.' I paused. 'The real thing was, I didn't miss a short one.' The point really only occurred to me as I said it.

'That's unlike you. You must have taken my advice.'

'Which was?'

'Don't worry about it. Just knock 'em in.'

'Quite.'

Over dinner I volunteered the same information to Celia.

'. . . And the thing was, darling, I didn't miss a single short one.'

'Well done, darling. Have some more parsnips.'

The thing about doing something easy well is that to begin with you take it for granted. Each occasion on its own demands no comment. Only as time goes by do you build up a reputation for excellence. This happened with my short putting.

It isn't as if I always won the monthly medal, but my handicap came down and my short putting was indeed excellent. Better than that, it was perfection. I never missed one.

Only gradually did I recognise the success I was having,

but as I did my golf moved up a gear, in every respect but most of all enjoyment. Gone was that sinking feeling of, Will I three-putt? Will I chip close and fluff the three-footer? Instead I walked on to the greens with ever-rising confidence, so that my long putting benefited too.

I don't know when this mood of near-euphoria began to sour, but I have to presume that deep in my psyche those cavalier words – 'I'd give anything never to miss a four-footer again' – were reverberating.

It was a day in late September when I began to grow really uneasy. Again I was playing with Alfred, Bob and Harry, as I'd done so often before. We were on the last green and I needed a four-footer to clinch the match. The wind had been blowing a gale all afternoon and the light was poor. It was a friendly and nothing stood on the result, but one likes to win.

I leant over the putt and wasted no time. Success had made me rapid. I took the clubhead back to hit the ball. At that moment the wind, which had momentarily eased, roared back with all the force the Channel can muster. I was pushed to one side, barged like a foot-baller, definitely an unfair challenge. My club was already in downward motion and there was no way I could make clean contact with the ball.

My club jabbed into the ground behind the ball, failing to make contact, or so it seemed. To my astonishment, and horror, the ball moved forward of its own volition and unerringly rolled firmly into the hole.

The Hell of Putting

'Well, you really can't miss, Jim,' said Bob over a pint. 'I was sure you had missed that last putt.'

I felt subdued, uneasy. 'So was I,' was all I said. I didn't hang around. Celia did not find me much company that evening.

The panic that had been rising took hold. A golfer's panic, drawn out over weeks of golf, but panic nevertheless.

The form my panic took was to try to miss short putts. I swung at the ball with my left hand. I looked up just as I played. I tapped it while looking in the other direction. I got an old blade putter, the sort I'd never been able to use, and swiped at the ball. I used the back of the putter, the toe, the heel. I topped it, I side-swiped at it, I jabbed at it, I dabbed at it. Come wind, rain and hail, slopes uphill, downhill, viciously from left to right, right to left. It was no good. I could not miss.

My sleep began to suffer and so did my digestion. I lost weight and much of my good humour. But my golf, no, that went from strength to strength. Celia spent more time in the garden, at the garden centre and with her friends. Our conversations became shorter and she began to seem as distracted as I was. I cannot say I was surprised when, in February, I found a note from Celia when I came home one Saturday evening, saying she had gone to stay with her mother. She did not think we were compatible any more.

My golf had moved on to an altogether higher plane.

The Captain's Cup was upon us and I was widely recognised to be in contention. I duly made my way through the field.

It was one of the few still, mild days at St Wilfrid's that I can remember that saw me on the first tee driving off against Bobby Gunn, alias 'Tommy', in the final.

I played well. So did Tommy. He should have given me three shots, but everyone said he was a bandit off three handicap. They said I was a bandit off seven. I had come down from fifteen in the course of hardly a year. We were playing level.

We slugged it out. He was three up at the turn, but he began to feel the pressure. He had a three-footer to keep his lead at the twelfth, but pushed it past to the right. He steadied but at the sixteenth I sank a ten-footer to get back another one, and again he missed from close at the seventeenth. We went to the last all square.

As I walked up the eighteenth after a steady drive down the middle I felt a warm glow. I had fought my way back into the match. The members were on the veranda, wooden-faced, but I could sense a current of appreciation. I had played well under pressure. Certainly, I had not had to sink any testing short putts, they had been 'tap-ins' or from further out, but I had that comforting certainty of success if tested.

I looked across to Tommy as he made his way to his ball. The spring had gone out of his stride. I could well imagine his frame of mind. He was saying a prayer. 'Oh,

God, please don't give me a four-footer.' He had no confidence left.

I hit my second short of the green. He put his second thirty feet from the pin. I chipped to within three feet.

His face was the picture of anguish. He knew he had to get down in two to halve the hole and stay in the match. But he had no confidence left in his short putting. He had to get close. The wish betrayed the act. He put his approach five feet past and missed the return.

I had a three-footer to win the Captain's Cup. I thought of Celia. I thought of my declining popularity in the clubhouse – Old Metronome I was known as, with a shade of bitterness. Alfred and Bob had made excuses to me a few months ago – they did not feel I was in their class any longer. But did I care? Hell, no! I was about to win the Captain's Cup, and deservedly.

I stood still for a while and looked up at the faces of the members looking down at me, not necessarily liking but respecting a damn good golfer with nerves of steel. And, as I stood, I reflected. Yes, it was worth it. I would give anything never to miss another four-footer or less. And I looked into my soul and I said to myself, 'Yes, Jim, you've given your soul. And it's worth it. I'm glad you've done it because you're going to sink this putt and win the Cup.'

I walked up to the marker, put down my ball. Took up my usual stance. I could not control the smile which spread across my face. Effortlessly, like a metronome, I hit the ball. It rolled towards the hole but drifted off line, caught the lip and spun out. I missed a four-footer on the first hole of the sudden-death play-off. I have hardly sunk a short putt since.

And Celia? Well, that's another story.